. . . but

GOD

can

...but

GOD

can

ROBERT V. OZMENT

FLEMING H. REVELL COMPANY

Library of Congress Catalog Card Number: 62-8593

Printed in the United States of America

1.1

FOR
MY MOTHER AND DADDY
*whose wise counsel, unceasing prayers
and Christian example left an indelible mark
on my life*

Introduction

"A Doctor of Philosophy with the common touch"—that is Robert V. Ozment. During the time he was attending and graduating from three universities, he also was in close touch with people. He mastered his subjects in the classrooms and also felt the heartbeat of the multitudes. He worked his way through school preaching in rural churches in the South, in city churches in the East, and even for a time lived on New York's famous Bowery.

After completing his work at Harvard and Boston University, he served as pastor of a large church in Havana, Cuba; later at a college church in Georgia, and is now the pastor of a leading church in Atlanta.

In . . . *but God can*, Dr. Ozment shows penetrating insight into eight important areas. He goes directly to the needs of mankind and applies to those needs the truths of God. Someone once said of a certain minister, "He seems to be always preaching to the man on the moon." As one sits under the ministry of Dr. Ozment, he is moved to say, "He is always preaching to me."

Some ministers feel called of God to lead in needed social reforms of their day, to use their powers especially against the sins of society. Some ministers are led to theological search and study. They enrich the treasury of man's knowledge. Other ministers feel it is their calling to devote themselves to what we think of as the personal or practical ministry. They help people find the way through the problems and trials of daily living. These chapters by Dr. Ozment are in the latter category. Whoever reads and digests this book will gain inspiration and understanding to live a more triumphant life.

For many years it has been my privilege to enjoy the friendship of this consecrated and brilliant young minister. I love and admire Bob very much, and I thank God for him.

CHARLES L. ALLEN

Contents

Contents

. . . but

GOD

can

1

TEMPTATION:

The Challenge and the Choice

TEMPTATION IS A traveling companion of every person who walks down the corridor of life. It has no regard for custom, race, or heritage. It cuddles up to the rich and the poor. It stands beside the intellectual giant as well as the illiterate; it travels with those who ride in royal coaches, and walks with the peasants. It snuggles up to the saint and grabs the hand of the avowed sinner. Temptation slights no race, it skips no generation. Wherever you find human life, you may be sure temptation is near.

There is a little phrase in the prayer our Lord taught His disciples that has always disturbed me. It is the part which reads: "And lead us not into temptation." What does this mean? Are we to assume that temptation is a part of the divine purpose? If so, is it proper for us to pray that God will save us from anything that fits into His divine scheme?

Just what do we mean when we pray: "And lead us not into temptation, but deliver us from evil"? The word "tempt" means to entice or seduce. We must dismiss at once the idea that God would induce or entice us to sin. I do not believe that God would ever seek to lead His children down a trail of moral disaster or chaos. It also appears wholly inconceivable seriously to entertain the thought that God would seek to draw us astray and in any way design a trap that would place the soul in jeopardy, and cause us to surrender our noble aspirations to beastly desires, or to switch our allegiance from the eternal to a passing pleasure. In the little Epistle of James we read, "Let no man say when he is tempted, I am tempted of God: for God cannot be tempted with evil, neither tempteth he any man: But every man is tempted, when he is drawn away of his own lust and enticed" (James 1:13-14).

Now I believe this about temptation: God leads us into temptation only in the sense that He has created a world in which temptation is inevitable. Even then, we must hasten to remember that out of these unavoidable temptations we can emerge as stronger Christians and more stalwart men and women in the faith.

Let us consider some possible interpretations of this baffling phrase, "And lead us not into temptation." First, the Greek word which is commonly translated *temptation* is, to say the least, confusing. It is exceedingly ambiguous. It could be translated to mean *trial,* or *test.* Therefore, it is altogether possible that Jesus taught His disciples to pray, "And lead us not into trial," or "And lead us not into spiritual tests."

Second, we could interpret this phrase to mean something akin to the first, yet different in degree. For example, it could mean this: Do not let us be exposed to situations in which we are likely to sin. Give us wisdom and spiritual insight to discern areas and situations which would cause us to stumble.

Finally, I do not believe we can lift a phrase out of its context and give it a wise and intelligent interpretation. We must read into its meaning the statement which precedes the phrase as well as that which follows.

Think with me about another prayer Jesus prayed. The scene was underneath the olive trees in the Garden of Gethsemane. Eight of Jesus' disciples were found just outside the garden engaged in friendly conversation. Peter, James, and John were deeper in the garden, only a few yards away from the Master, fast asleep. Jesus was faced with the greatest struggle of His entire career. He was lying stretched out, His face to the ground, His fingers buried deep in the dirt. The silence gave way to His agonizing prayer: "Oh my Father, if it be possible, let this cup pass from me." Now, if Jesus had ended His prayer at this point, we would interpret it thus: Take away this cruel cross; get Me out of this horrible situation; provide some legitimate substitute for the cross; create a morally acceptable detour around this dreadful experience. But the prayer did not end there. Jesus took no more than a short breath before He was praying again. The very next phrase reads: "Nevertheless not as I will, but as thou wilt" (Matthew 26:39).

The latter prayerful plea changes the picture. It throws a different light on the whole scene. Jesus was human enough to want to avoid the cross, yet He was divine enough to endure it if God had provided no alternate route. The scene is no longer that of Christ praying for an easy path. Now, Jesus is praying, "Oh God, if the cross cannot be removed, give me the strength to face it and remain faithful. Deliver me from the evil possibilities of this ugly cross."

Let us again turn our attention to the phrase, "And lead us not into temptation." The phrase preceding it reads: "And forgive us our debts, as we forgive our debtors." Here we truly see a picture of a man at prayer. He has just prayed for and has received God's divine forgiveness of his past sins. In an effort to remain in this forgiven relationship, in an effort to keep his soul clean, in an effort to follow faithfully he prays: "And lead us not into temptation." He does not end his prayer here, but continues, "but deliver us from evil." Is not this a parallel of the prayer Jesus prayed in the garden? Temptation, like the cross, is inevitable. We cannot avoid it. Therefore, we can only pray, "If temptation cannot be removed, when life places us in the midst of temptation, deliver us from its evil clutches. Keep us from yielding. Keep us faithful, even in the face of life's strongest temptations." I believe a true interpretation of this baffling portion of our Lord's prayer might read as follows: "Lord, when temptation is near, keep my soul from becoming contaminated; deliver me safely out of the possible evil that is involved."

In any consideration of temptation, we must take into account the following two facts. First, temptation is an inevitable certainty. A man or woman can no more live without facing temptation than one can breath without lungs. Second, God has endowed human personality with a free nature. That is to say, man has in life a freedom of choice. He can choose to court temptation, play with it, cultivate its friendship, become engaged in its evil scheme, and eventually become trapped in its morally degrading web.

The very fact that temptation exists and, further, that man is free to choose, opens the gate to possible moral disaster. This is not strange, because all of life is lived within certain unalterable laws.

If you stand on a bridge and drop your car keys over the deep chasm below, the keys will be drawn to the bottom by the force of gravitation. One of the most common mathematical laws is illustrated in the fact that two plus two equals four.

Life is also governed by spiritual laws. No man can defy the laws of God and enjoy a large measure of spiritual peace and confidence. To do so is as incongruous as trying to mix water and gasoline. In view of inevitable temptation and man's freedom, here is a spiritual law which we ought to remember: God will give us the necessary moral fortitude to conquer and to be victorious over temptation.

Let me suggest some things that can be said about temptation, no matter in what form it appears.

1. God is both aware that we are being tempted and He is present during periods of temptation. He stands near to encourage us to take the right turn, and to urge us to make the right choice.

Paul wrote to the church at Corinth and said two significant things about temptation. First, he assured the Corinthians that God would never allow them to be tempted beyond their ability to remain true and faithful. That is to say, if we apply Paul's writings to our own situations, if we yield to temptation, we sin and become estranged from God by our own choosing. We may try to justify our actions by logic and rationalizations, but to yield to temptation is a sign of human weakness and not a deficiency in divine power. Nathaniel Willis wrote, "No degree of temptation justifies any degree of sin."

In a second statement to the people of Corinth, Paul expressed in unequivocal terms his belief that God provides a way through which we may safely pass during temptations. "God," wrote Paul, "will with the temptation also make a way to escape, that ye may be able to bear it" (I Corinthians 10:13). Paul did not say that God would build a detour around temptations. God will never curb human desires. He will give us power to control them, and He will help us to consecrate them, but He will never remove them. God promises us that He will give us strength to overcome temptation and open a door whereby we may escape.

A few weeks ago, a successful businessman came to see me. He had been a faithful member of a church in another state. In his spiritual life he had developed a vital and wonderful relationship with God. He was promoted and moved to our city. His position almost demanded social drinking. He lived by the philosophy that anything that caused so much hardship and sorrow as alcohol was morally wrong. He was nervous and tense.

One day he went to the hospital for a physical checkup. The doctor told him he should quit drinking. "Now," he said, "I've got an excuse and I have quit drinking. When my friends offer me a drink, I simply tell them the doctor has ordered me to stop."

I told my visitor about another man I know who is the president of his company. There was a time in this man's life when he drank excessively. He finally came to the conclusion that drinking was ruining his life; therefore, he quit. He is still tempted to drink when his old friends and associates are around, but God has opened a door that permits him to escape during these temptations. He simply says, "No, thank you, I don't drink any more." God opened for him the door of courage. It takes a lot of courage for this man to say what he does, but God has given him that courage.

When we are tempted, God will furnish an open door by which we can escape. It may be the door of courage, or the door of common sense. It may be the door of fair play, the application of the old adage "Do unto others as you would have them do unto you."

Think about the lonely hours Jesus spent in the Garden of Gethsemane on the night of the arrest. These were difficult hours for the Master. He was lonely, yet not alone; His soul was protected by His overwhelming desire to please His Father. His commitment to God's will saved Him. Do you suppose Jesus was tempted? I think so. Surely, He was tempted to escape. The shadow of an ugly cross must have covered His soul with mystery and despair. His soul was troubled, He trembled with fear. In this dark hour Jesus must have said to Himself, "I could run. I could get the disciples together and get out of Jerusalem. We could go back to Capernaum and work around the shores of Galilee. It was around the shores of Galilee that I healed Peter's mother-in-law, the lepers, and many others. We will be among friends. They will love and appreciate us."

During Jesus' mighty struggle in the garden, God came upon the scene. Above the rustle of the olive leaves, and beyond the clamor of personal desire, Jesus heard the voice of God. I think God must have said something like this, "My son, be not afraid. I am with you.

The cross is cruel. It will be humiliating and painful. But it will stand for eternity as a symbol of my love for man. It will inspire and challenge the human family as long as men march across the stage of life. By the cross, men will be lifted from their lives of spiritual poverty to the riches of my grace. From the cross there will flow an unceasing stream of fresh and healing water, where thirsty men and women, boys and girls, may quench the deep thirst of their souls. Go to the cross, my son. I will open a door of love through which you may pass and not be polluted by the evil this temptation suggests."

Jesus passed through the door of love that night in the garden. He loved God with all His heart and soul and mind. He loved an undeserving humanity even more than He loved Himself. He was no longer tempted to run. God opened a door for Him.

2. Temptation is only an invitation to sin. Within itself, it is neither good nor evil. It brings neither honor nor shame. It was William Shakespeare who said, "It is one thing to be tempted, and another thing to fall." No man is ever divinely condemned by meeting temptation; we are condemned only when we make out of temptation a personal friend. Temptations from without can never harm the soul unless there is an overpowering and corresponding desire within. I like the first verse of an old hymn which was written by H. R. Palmer:

> Yield not to temptation
> For yielding is sin;
> Each victory will help you
> Some other to win;
> Fight manfully onward,
> Dark passions subdue;
> Look ever to Jesus
> He'll carry you through.

3. Temptation serves, I believe, as a testing ground for the soul. Some time ago I visited a factory where huge airplanes are manufactured. I was especially interested in the "endurance tests" the planes had to undergo. Undue stress and strain were administered to the plane, the purpose being to make the plane safe and to determine its limitations. Temptations sometimes try our strength and

18

they reveal unto God something about our dependability or unworthiness, as the case may be.

Temptation in life is some ways like the testing of a ship. A ship cannot be tested if anchored safely in the harbor of calm and protected water. Yet send this ship on a voyage, and in the middle of the ocean it encounters a great storm. The ship did not seek the storm; the storm is the result of certain atmospheric conditions. Nevertheless, the storm would try the strength of the ship and test the skill of the captain.

The tests of life are like that. There are times when we find ourselves surrounded by the mighty waves of temptation. We do not seek them. They are the result of conditions beyond our control. Nevertheless, these temptations challenge our spiritual strength and test our ability to mount the mighty waves of temptation and sail toward some noble and worthy harbor. One of my favorite little poems was written by R. L. Sharpe:

> Isn't it strange
> That princes and kings,
> And clowns that caper
> In sawdust rings,
> And common people
> Like you and me
> Are builders for eternity?
>
> Each is given a bag of tools,
> A shapeless mass,
> A book of rules;
> And each must make,
> Ere life is flown,
> A stumbling-block
> Or a stepping-stone.

Our ability to choose is a part of the tools, and our temptations represent a part of the shapeless mass out of which we will either make "a stumbling-block or a stepping-stone."

4. Temptation is a battleground upon which man's selfishness challenges God's divine will. Temptation is a conflict between that which I want to do and that which I know I ought to do.

Man is in grave danger at this point in life. We have been endowed with great strength. We can succeed in getting our way in life when we face many of life's temptations. Herein lies the danger. God will permit us to follow our foolish and selfish ways, rather than to restrict our freedom and force His will and wisdom upon us. We have seen people ruin their lives by insistence on getting their own way in life. They yield to one temptation after another. They satisfy one sinful desire after another until they find they have cast themselves on the scrap pile of broken dreams and empty hopes.

The challenge belongs to you and me. The decision is ours to make. Will we let Christ be at the center of life? No one can make this decision for us. We make it over and over again when we face temptation. May God help us to give Him first place.

The old saying, "There are two sides to everything," is certainly true regarding temptation. No discussion of this subject would be inclusive unless we look at both sides. Usually, when we think of temptation we think of some evil trap set for the righteous. However, there are also temptations, or righteous impulses—call them what you will—which emerge quite naturally along the trail of life. There are times in every life when we are overwhelmed with an inner longing to live on a higher plane. God places within us a feeling of discontent with the petty, mediocre, and lewd. He keeps tempting us to leave the low road and travel the high way that leads to noble living.

Let us never stifle the temptation that incites righteousness. Poverty on the part of our neighbors tempts us to do something about it. Injustice stirs us to action. Wrong and suffering will not permit the sensitive soul to rest until some effort has been exerted to right the wrong and to relieve the pain. Such noble and righteous temptations flow from the heart of God through the stream of humanity.

Here is a strange note about temptation. The saint is far more sensitive and is aware of more temptations than those who are spiritually less mature. Think about this. The most difficult plateau upon which mortal feet can walk is the spiritual peak of sainthood. Some persons who are only half-dedicated to God dream about the ease and uninterrupted life of the saint. Yet a casual study of the lives of the saints tells us that they are not tempted less than others. A saintly person's keen perception of God's will keeps him constantly in the arena of temptation.

The average man measures his actions by what is socially acceptable; the saint measures his by divine standards. The average person is content to live in the boundaries of respectability; the saint is never quite satisfied with his life. The average man prays spasmodically; he repents occasionally. The saint marches through life with a prayer on his lips and unceasing repentance in his heart. The average man feels the need of God only during a crisis. The saint lives constantly in an awareness of his utter dependence upon God.

Once Paul wrote to the church at Corinth indicating his fervent desire to visit there. In Corinth he would get some needed rest. He would be among friends and they would care for his needs. In Ephesus, however, he saw a great opportunity to expand the boundaries of the Kingdom. He forgot himself and his wishes and thought only of God's will. He was tempted to go, but found the courage to stay. Paul wrote, "There are many adversaries" in Ephesus. Now, no one would have criticized Paul for continuing toward Corinth, which was a part of his plans. The halfhearted person would not have been aware of temptation at this juncture. But Paul, who had dedicated and conquered his desire for soft, comfortable living, recognized that his wish to visit Corinth was in opposition to a door of opportunity that had been opened.

The mountain peak of sainthood is not beyond the long and persistent arm of temptation. The saint must constantly crucify his opinions, his preferences, his tastes, and his will. Temptation appeals to man's selfishness. It comes in many forms. Let me suggest four.

1. Temptation attacks the powerful urges of our physical bodies. We have certain responsibilities toward this body. It makes continued demands upon us. It demands food, air, and water, as well as other things. Now, it would be foolish to assume that any kind of food is sufficient. Any good doctor or dietitian will tell you that it is not the amount of food you eat that counts as much as it is the type of food you eat. It is not satisfactory to give your body unclean air; it must be reasonably pure. We spend uncounted millions of dollars each year in an effort to purify the water we drink. The body could not survive on polluted water. These simple facts

about the demands of our bodies should reveal to us some important truths: namely, the body needs constant care, regular attention, and intelligent management. It is common knowledge to the refined soul that many demands of the body must be curbed, controlled, and mastered.

Consider the sex instinct, for example; it is one of the most powerful urges of life. To live by the philosophy that it must be satisfied on our own terms will ruin civilization and bring the soul to moral chaos. This desire, like many other desires, must be kept under constant guard and wise supervision. The sex life of an individual must be consecrated and satisfied only in the framework of God's eternal will.

The Bible tells us that after the baptism of Jesus, He fasted forty days and forty nights. "And when the tempter came to him, he said, If thou be the Son of God, command that these stones be made bread" (Matthew 4:3). This temptation represents a real struggle, a struggle between a weary soul and the power of evil. Jesus must have said to Himself, "I cannot fail. To yield would be to lose everything." This temptation appears to be an innocent one; Jesus was hungry. It is no sin either to be hungry or to satisfy this basic need in life. Jesus' friends were hungry, and our Lord was well aware of the fact that men suffered in poverty because of the heavy burden of the Roman taxes. The tempter must have emphasized the hunger of Jesus, and I suspect he said, "If thou be the Son of God, command that these stones be made bread. Feed the hungry; help wipe out some of this poverty." But Jesus would not be tricked. He was weak from fasting, but He was spiritually alert.

Jesus' temptation born of hunger goes deeper than simply feeding an empty stomach. It was an occasion to scar a pure soul; it was a temptation to doubt God. Jesus could have turned stones to bread, but in doing so He would have been saying, "I must prove to Myself that I am truly God's Son." The tempter began, "If thou be the Son of God. . . ." Jesus knew He was the Son of God. He would not doubt that for a single minute.

The temptation to ease His hunger encouraged Jesus to misuse the power of God. He was hungry, and He needed to eat; therefore, He was tempted to use His power to satisfy His own personal need. This He would not do. When others were starving, they could not

22

turn stones to bread and satisfy their inner craving for food; neither would Jesus do so to satisfy His hunger. Jesus taught a lesson we need to learn as He answered the tempter, "It is written, Man shall not live by bread alone, but by every word that proceedeth out of the mouth of God" (Matthew 4:4).

For the individual, it is not enough to own two cars and belong to the country club. Happiness does not come from drinking out of sparkling crystal or eating with glittering silver. We must not live for things that pass away. We need to anchor our hopes upon things eternal. The abundant life is found not in things, but in obeying the commands of God.

For the nation, it is not sufficient to have more missiles, muscles, and satellites. If we survive and live together in peace, we must live by understanding, forgiveness, and respect for the dignity of man.

2. Temptation spurs man's desire for popularity. We all have the desire to be "somebody." In the New Testament there is a very interesting story of an ambitious mother. She asked Jesus to give her two sons a favored place in the Kingdom.

The desire to be popular must be guided. There is nothing wrong with the desire to be a congenial, well-thought-of and popular person. In fact, I think Jesus wanted this kind of relationship with people. The important question we need to ask is this, "What will it cost us to gain popularity?" If we must lose our self-respect, degrade our souls, or yield to earthly temptations, then popularity is too costly.

When Jesus was tempted to jump from the pinnacle of the temple, He must have thought of the effect this would have on the crowd. Surely this would gain Him a great following. Such a stunt would prove to the crowd that Jesus not only trusted God, but in this exhibition men could see the power of God at work. Yet Jesus knew that the Kingdom of God would not come out of some miracle, but would grow gradually. It would come not because of the spectacular, but as the result of hearts and minds being captured by His unswerving loyalty to God, His unceasing love to man, and His unwavering faith in the goodness and wisdom of God.

3. Man's thirst for power is another form of temptation with which we must deal. Power rightly used will bring honor and progress. Power used selfishly brings dishonor, shame, and misery

23

beyond man's ability to imagine. The greatest tragedies ever to befall the human race have come as the result of men who let power corrupt their sense of man's worth. Because ungodly men have stood at the helm of governments, civilizations have been destroyed, talents squandered, justice trampled, and unnumbered millions have entered prematurely into the silent halls of death.

The third temptation of our Lord was probably the greatest crisis He faced until the night of His arrest. The tempter took Jesus to the peak of a high mountain; here, he showed Him all the kingdoms of the world and asked for a compromise. "All these things will I give thee, if thou wilt fall down and worship me" (Matthew 4:9).

Evil has a way of taking what it can get. If it cannot get all of a man's devotion, it will endeavor to get a little. Consider the man who has experienced the evils and heartaches of alcohol. With the help of God he stops drinking. The tempter does not urge him to get drunk; he knows this approach will not work. He simply says, "Just take one drink. What harm can that do? Just take one to be sociable." This is the compromise.

As Jesus surveyed the countryside from the top of the mountain where He had been bidden by the tempter, His mind must have been full of thoughts of how much He wanted the kingdoms that were spread out below. The Hebrews had been ruthlessly treated for decade after decade; at the very time of the temptation, Roman soldiers marched in every town of any size. Jesus must have reviewed His purpose in life. He decided once and for all that He must work with His Father if a new Kingdom were to be ushered into the pagan world. He fully committed Himself to walk under the sway of God's will. Jesus never misused His power; He never compromised with evil. He was always ready to say, "Thy will be done." He repeated again and again that He had come to do the work of His Father.

4. Our desire for material things is another form of temptation that we need to conquer. Suppose someone were to ask you to name the one thing among your possessions that you consider priceless. What would you name? You may have some expensive jewels, or antiques. Even if these objects could not be replaced, there is something more valuable. When I look at my own situation in the

24

light of this question, I say without hesitation that my little son is the most important thing that has been entrusted to my care. I don't know of anything on the face of the earth that excels in importance over life. It may denote a little egotism on the part of man to feel that he is so significant, yet the writer of the story of creation reminds us that human personality is made in the image of God.

In our busy pace of living it is easy to allow our goals to be mixed and our purposes confused. I have talked to many people who have let this happen. Peter let it happen in his life. Jesus told His disciples that He would be rejected by the elders and scribes, that He would be killed by ruthless and indifferent men. Peter interrupted at this point. According to the Bible, he began to rebuke Jesus. I can imagine Peter's saying something like this, "Master, this will not happen. No one will dare lay a hand on You. I will take the personal responsibility to see that it does not happen. You can count upon me to protect You with my very life."

Then Jesus spoke to Peter, saying, "Thou savourest not the things that be of God, but the things that be of men" (Mark 8:33). Jesus was saying to Peter, "I know you mean well, but you are confused. You have placed your own wishes and hopes above the will and wisdom of God."

When Jesus saw the shadow of the cross in the Garden of Gethsemane, He cautioned His disciples. They were in danger of deserting Him in His time of need and, thereby, deserting themselves. Jesus knew the disciples would be tempted to run. Therefore, He said to the three sleeping disciples, "Watch ye and pray, lest ye enter into temptation. The spirit truly is ready, but the flesh is weak" (Mark 14:38).

Let us be determined not to court temptation. Many people find themselves engaged in a mighty struggle with temptation simply because they have opened the door and invited it to come in for a visit. For instance, let us think of the businessman who intends to be honest in filling out his expense account, but who soon discovers his associates are taking advantage of the company. The tempter whispers, "Go ahead, it's only a few dollars." The businessman rejects the suggestion. But the tempter comes again, "You work as hard

25

as the others. Everybody else is doing it. You might as well get your share." He yields.

There are five questions which we ought to ask ourselves in the presence of temptation.

1. If I engage in this activity, will it degrade human personality? Human personality at its best is noble. It is sacred. It shines with a spiritual lustre that denotes divine worth. It is never ashamed. When temptation sends us an invitation, we ought, before we accept, to be certain that we will emerge from the experience with a high regard for ourselves. Jesus must have asked Himself this question as He faced temptation, "Will I be less than what God expects of Me if I turn stones to bread, jump from the pinnacle, or worship Satan?" The answer came back strong and clear, "Yes." If after objective scrutiny, you get an affirmative answer to the question of degrading personality, reject the invitation.

2. Another question by which we can test temptation is this, "Where will it lead me?" Every deed is a step leading somewhere. It may be toward the land of gladness and holy living or it could be in the direction of misery and moral degradation.

Using one curse word will not make you an habitual user of profanity; it is only one short step in that direction. Betting on one race horse will not make you a gambling addict; it simply opens the door to that possibility. No one ever became an alcoholic by sipping one cocktail; on the other hand, there are no alcoholics who have never taken the first drink. Unless the activity sends us on the road that leads to worthy habits, we ought to conquer the temptation.

3. Still another question we should consider in the presence of temptation is this, "Will my engaging in this activity cause another to stumble?" We do not live unto ourselves. I believe God holds us responsible for our influence upon other people. In the light of the life and death of our Lord, we have come to believe that the answer to that ancient question, "Am I my brother's keeper?" is definitely "Yes."

We must not forget that our relationship with others will, in no small measure, determine our relationship with God. The two cannot be divorced. The Christian attitude is to shun temptation if the results would adversely affect another.

4. Then, we ought to examine temptation in the light of this question, "Would I be willing to permit those I love most to enter into this activity?" We may be sure that anything that would not be good for those we love would not be good for us. One of the greatest commandments, according to Jesus, is this: "Thou shalt love thy neighbour as thyself" (Mark 12:31). In view of the question under consideration we could turn this commandment around and be determined to love ourselves as much as we love others.

5. Finally, let us give this acid test to the temptations we face: "If I yield to this temptation, will it meet the standard of God's will for my life?" In all His relationships Jesus lived by the rule, "Not my will, but thine be done."

Remember two things about temptation: First, you cannot escape it; second, God will give you the power to be victorious and overcome the strongest and most insistent temptations.

2 BURDENS:
Hold Fast to the Eternal

ON MY DESK there is a stack of letters that have come to me during the past few months. In a way, these letters are very special to me; they represent the heartaches, broken dreams, crushed hopes, wasted lives, and, in general, the tremendously heavy burdens the writers have been called upon to shoulder. In reading these letters I have noticed that this little phrase, "Please pray for me," appears in each of them.

Consider, for instance, this letter: a woman writes, "I have been in the hospital for over two long years. I have known many sleepless nights and at times the pain is almost unbearable. Please pray that God will give me strength to remain a faithful disciple until the end."

Another person writes, "My wife and I have tried to live a good life; we have always gone to church and have done everything we knew that a Christian ought to do. In spite of this, our only son has been stricken with an incurable disease. He is now at the point of death. Please pray for us. I am about to lose my faith in God. I cannot understand why God let this happen to us. Could you give me the answer to the question *why?*"

Now the question *why* is exceedingly difficult to answer. It is much easier to answer other questions, such as: when did it happen? where did it happen? how did it happen? Human wisdom can usually supply the answers to the latter questions. Only God will be able to give us an answer to the *why* of the baffling and sometimes agonizing experiences that cause many of us to cry out in utter desperation.

When I was a freshmen in college I was appointed to serve six rural churches in the beautiful mountains of western North Carolina. Soon after I arrived, someone asked me to visit a sick member of one of the little churches for which I had been given the responsibility. I was given a little of the man's background: he was almost fifty years old, and he had spent the last twenty years of his life in one room, flat on his back. I was frightened at the thought of seeing this man. The thought that came to my mind was this: Suppose he should ask me this question, "Why did this happen to me?" What would I say? Would I be adequately prepared to represent God in a situation such as this? I must admit that I felt rather insecure. I prayed that God would put the words in my mouth that should be expressed in case the sick man questioned me.

My fears subsided as I entered the house, and they vanished completely as I walked into the room. I could see the faint shadow of a smile across his pain-racked face. "Come on in, Preacher," he said. "I am glad to see you." We talked for a long while and before I left he said something like this to me, "Twenty years in this little room is a long time. There are times when I feel like screaming because the pain is so intense. But God helps me through each day. I am not complaining, but a man cannot help but wonder at times why he must bear such a heavy load. Then, I think of Christ. He never asked *why*. He only asked God for strength to live life to its fullest. When you come to think about it, twenty years is a mighty short time compared to eternity. Somehow, I know that I was born, not for a few years of suffering, but for eternity. I have stopped asking *why*—I just pray for the courage and strength to be faithful."

I left that room with a new song upon my lips. I said to myself, "I may never understand why some people struggle under the weight of many burdens, but I know God stands in the shadows keeping watch over His own. No man could stay in a little twelve-by-fourteen room for twenty years and grow such a radiant spirit unless God is with him."

When we learn to carry our burdens, it seems so unnecessary to find the answer to the question *why*. Jesus had some questions in

His mind as He looked at Calvary from the Garden of Gethsemane. ". . . Now is my soul troubled," said Jesus, "and what shall I say?" (John 12:27). Was Jesus trying to understand the cross? Was He asking God to tell Him *why?* Whatever the reason, Jesus did not hesitate for long. He whispered to His Father, "Father, glorify thy name . . ." (John 12:28).

The miracle of *how* stands at the center of the stage when we accept our burdens. How can one shoulder the heavy load and stand with a noble spirit and proclaim as his daily litany the words of the psalmist, "The Lord is good to all: and his tender mercies are over all his works" (Psalm 145:9). The answer is found when we come to know the truth of the words of Moses as he blessed the twelve tribes of Israel before his death. "The eternal God is thy refuge, and underneath are the everlasting arms . . ." (Deuteronomy 33:27). When we feel the presence of God and know that His strong arms are around us, we have found the source of strength that enables us to walk through the dark nights toward the dawn with an unwavering faith in both His goodness and His wisdom.

The questions which keep raising their heads in many minds are these: Does God send the storms of life; and, are these heavy burdens divinely appointed? These questions have a magnitude that is far-reaching. They are important and need to be analyzed.

There are those who contend that God sends the storms of life and causes the waves to beat upon the sides of our little ships. These storms, they reason, are not without a divine purpose; they come in order to make us look at our lives and alter our courses and head toward some noble harbor. These people give sustenance to the idea that we must walk across the chasm of sorrow, suffering, and disappointment before we reach the summit of our spiritual development.

One of the most thought-provoking incidents in the New Testament is the story of the blind man who had never seen a lovely flower, the blue sky, or a majestic sunrise. He was born blind. The disciples asked Jesus this question, ". . . who did sin, this man, or his parents . . ?" (John 9:2). They took for granted that the blindness was payment for either the man's own sins or the mistakes of his parents. This is clear evidence of the early conception that man's burdens were the fruits of evil living. It should go without saying that many of our heavy burdens are due to our own selfish ways. Some are due to our neglect. However, we cannot account for all the difficulties we encounter by writing them off as the result of sin.

Jesus spoke quickly and clearly after the disciples posed the question as to whether the blind man's handicap was due to somebody's sin. ". . . Neither hath this man sinned," said Jesus, "nor his parents . . ." (John 9:3). There can be no doubt in our minds that many of our burdens come from sources other than sin.

The next remark Jesus made gives some evidence to the position held by many people that God is directly responsible for sending our burdens in order for us to achieve a higher good. That is to say, the burdens we bear are mere training exercises that will enable us to become stronger in the faith and more effective in our Christian witness. However, this does not explain the many experiences people endure that tend to drive them away from God. Jesus indicated that the man in question was born blind for a divine purpose. He is blind in order ". . . that the works of God should be made manifest in him" (John 9:3). How shall we interpret this baffling remark of our Lord? First, we can interpret the statement of Jesus to mean that the man's burden of blindness was sent to him directly from God's throne. Therefore, he is blind according to a divine order and God will be glorified through his blindness. This would be a simple answer to all the burdens, heartaches, and suffering we feel in life. In days of agonizing pain and crushing sorrow we could explain them by saying, "God has given them to us for a divine purpose." This view satisfies some people, but it leaves me with an even greater conflict.

How can I reconcile the love, goodness, and mercy of God with so much suffering in the world? The innocent suffer; some enter this life and suffer from the door of birth to the door of death.

I stood, some months ago, by the bed of a little seven-year-old girl. She had a smile on her face, but an ugly disease was gradually sapping her strength and would eventually take her life. Medical science, up to this time, has not found the answer to this problem. One day scientists will conquer this disease, but it will be too late for this little girl. I could neither satisfy myself nor the grief-stricken parents by saying, "Don't worry about this, God sent this disease and some-

31

thing good will come out of it." I do not doubt for one minute that God can transform all our burdens and as a result of His presence and power make something good out of them; on the other hand, I fail to see God as the instigator of many tragedies that men experience.

Jesus taught us that God is like a good shepherd. Now, a good shepherd loves his sheep. He counts them at the end of the day to be sure that all of them are safely in the shelter he has provided. He checks each sheep to see if it has wounds that need his attention. If he discovers one sheep missing from the fold, he returns to the pasture in search for the lost. The shepherd may be weary, but he refuses to think of himself; he thinks only of the welfare of his sheep. When he finds the lost sheep, he gently lifts it to his shoulders and carefully takes it to the fold. Now, I believe God is like that.

In the course of a week I go in and out of many hospitals and see many people with burdens that are almost unbearable. I am forced to conclude and say with Plato, "Of our troubles we must seek some other cause than God."

Second, we can interpret the statement of Jesus to mean that without this man's blindness the glory of God could not be made manifest in him. That is to say, God did not send the burden to him; he is blind because of other circumstances. However, because of his blindness and Christian spirit, God will be glorified. In this situation man's weakness gives expression to God's strength and greatness. The man's blindness made him the object of a great miracle. God could not have used a man with twenty-twenty vision to manifest His glory in this way. This is a truth we forget or fail to see at all when we travel under the load of heavy burdens. It is conceivable that God can use us with greater effectiveness when we walk under the shadow of sorrow and disappointment. Most people will be remembered not because of the ease with which they sailed the sea of life, but because of the storms they faced and the struggles over which they became conquerors. This has been true many times.

I know a man who will be an inspiration to his friends as long as they live and remember him. He suffered more than any other person I have ever been privileged to know. For month after month he endured excruciating pain. Yet, in all of this, he waved high the flag of faith. No one could look at him even in his dying days and not be able to see that he was victorious. It was not play-acting; men do not play-act when the certain hands of death are on the scene. That man's gentle spirit, his kind thoughts, his unwavering courage, his unrelenting patience, his unflinching belief in God's unceasing love and infinite wisdom will serve to remind others that God will help His children to live above the burdens of life.

Think of David Livingstone. He spent thirty-three long years in the jungles of Africa. He broke away from those he loved in order to tell Africa's native people about God's love. Several times Livingstone barely escaped death, but this did not discourage him. Injustice and sin stalked the earth and he dedicated himself to replace man's ignorance with knowledge; man's suspicion with understanding; and man's hate with boundless love. Livingstone traveled through the jungles of Africa with a few black friends proclaiming the goodness of God. His body was weak from sickness, yet he bound up the wounds of others, started a school, and planned a church. He never retreated; he died on duty, and in recognition of his courageous missionary work against such death-defying odds the British empire saw to it that Livingstone's abused body was laid to rest in Westminster Abbey.

David Livingstone's bruised body and heavy burdens have caused many young missionaries to light their torches of faith and travel to the corners of the earth to tell others about the love of Christ. Had Livingstone refused to take God's hand and fight to his death under the weight of such opposition, God's glory could not have been reflected in him.

I know there is a reason behind the burdens we bear, and frequently we do not understand that reason. The source of our burdens lies sometimes within ourselves. This is true, even though we may be ignorant of the cause. Then, we bear some burdens because we are the victims of circumstances beyond our control. Try as we may, there is absolutely nothing we can do to change the situation. Finally, I would be willing to admit that in the great wisdom of God He may lead us down a rough road where there are many burdens. If this be the case, we are assured of the victory through the power of God even before the journey begins.

Hanna Smith lived by this philosophy. Sometimes the Good Shepherd leads us in pastures not of our own choosing. We find there opposition and earthly trials. When God leads us in a situation such as this, we will grow and become strong. There may be times when He feels that it is best to lead us not by the still waters, but beside boisterous waves and streams of sorrow and troubled waters. Even here, He will give us courage to lie down beside these waters and receive from them a spiritual blessing. "The Shepherd," writes Hanna Smith, "knows what pastures are best for his sheep, and they must not question nor doubt, but trustingly follow him."

When our burdens cast a shadow of confusion over our souls, we should remember the wise words of the writer of the Proverbs, "Trust in the Lord with all thine heart; and lean not unto thine own understanding. In all thy ways acknowledge him, and he shall direct thy paths" (Proverbs 3:5, 6).

There is an old hymn I like to sing. The Lord did not give me much talent in the area of singing, but I enjoy trying. E. W. Blandly wrote this hymn and the chorus ought to be the theme song of every Christian. It is an expression of complete trust in God. The chorus goes something like this:

> Where He leads me I will follow,
> Where He leads me I will follow,
> Where He leads me I will follow,
> I'll go with Him, with Him all the way.

When we come to the place in life where we trust Him unreservedly, the burdens of life are lifted. It matters not how many troubled waters cover our souls, life will be both beautiful and abundant. God will see to that.

Let us look at Calvary; it is a cruel and ugly scene. The taunts of evil men, the slurs of the crowd, and the indifference of a host of people are sufficient enough to make a sensitive man sick at his stomach. At the center of the stage, yea, even at the center of history, there is a stalwart Man, weary with the burdens of the world. The spirit of this Man demands our attention. He is exhausted; He looks defeated; yet, He is kind and gentle. His heart seems to go out to the crowd. His lips move slowly, as if He is praying. The rough soldiers carry out their orders: steel spikes are driven through Christ's hands and feet; His side is pierced. The blood gushes down

His legs and drips to the ground from the ends of His toes. A crown of sharp thorns is pressed onto His head. His body is racked with pain. Finally, His strength is gone; life ebbs away; He draws His last breath and dies.

What a horrible sight! Here was the only Man who ever lived without participating in the evil of the world. His life was spotless, His hands were clean, His heart was pure. Yet, God was glorified on Calvary more than at any other place in history. God took this ugly picture of His Son, struggling under the heaviest burden that the human mind is capable of imagining, and made out of it the most magnificent expression of God's love, concern, and forgiveness of mankind.

Thank God there are people who permit their burdens to be used to speak of God's love rather than to cast a shadow of doubt and skepticism over the lives of those who watch us struggle in the arena.

When Moses began the exciting and challenging task of releasing the Hebrews from slavery in Egypt and leading them to the Promised Land, God gave him some clear instructions. First, God assured Moses that he could accomplish such a great feat. "Come now therefore, and I will send thee unto Pharaoh, that thou mayest bring forth my people the children of Israel out of Egypt" (Exodus 3:10). God expected Moses to succeed. He knew Moses could do the job. He did not say, "I want you to go and try to deliver the Hebrews." God sent him to "bring them forth." Second, God assured Moses that He would be with him. No man ever walks down the road of life by himself. God is always near to give strength. God said to Moses, ". . . I will be with thee . . ." (Exodus 3:12). Finally, God promised to show Moses what to do and to teach him what to say. The Lord said to Moses, "I . . . will teach you what ye shall do" (Exodus 4:15).

Sometimes, perhaps by circumstances or perhaps by divine orders, life has a way of pushing us into a corner. The cares and burdens of life press hard upon our souls. Our strength at its best becomes weak; our courage at its height fails, and suddenly we become aware of our miserable plight. Everyone who reads these lines must have sailed down the river of crushed hopes, broken dreams, and unrealized aspirations. Could we not all say that there are times when life is not as fruitful as we had expected. Life is like an electronic computer; if you get the right answers, you must feed it the correct informa-

35

tion. The harvest we garner from life is completely dependent upon the seed we plant and the virtues we cultivate.

What shall we do when we find our burdens more than we can bear alone? Do you recall these words of Washington Gladden?

> In the bitter waves of woe,
> Beaten and tossed about
> By the sullen winds that blow
> From the desolate shores of doubt,
> When the anchors that faith has cast
> Are dragging in the gale,
> I am quietly holding fast
> To the things that cannot fail.

When burdens are heavy, I can at least do this: I can hold fast to the things that cannot fail. But what are the things that cannot fail? Let me suggest three things to which we can anchor our hopes during the days when burdens press upon us.

1. God knows that we can face all of life and be victorious. He never places us in a hopeless situation. We may stumble and fall, but God will provide the strength for us to get up and walk again. If we fall under the weight of heavy burdens and give up the struggle, it is not God's fault, it is our own.

2. We can hold fast to this eternal truth: God walks down the path of life with us. We are never alone.

The *Saturday Evening Post* published a story entitled "The Marvelous Mayos." In this story the writer tells about a patient who went to the Mayo Clinic for a physical check-up. After the examination, Dr. Charles W. Mayo frightened his patient when he gave his verdict: "You need an operation immediately."

The patient nervously twisted her hands and remarked, "But I'll be all alone."

Dr. Mayo gently tapped her on the hand and said, "No you won't, I'll be with you."

This very thing happened to Moses. He was afraid; he thought his task was beyond his own strength, and he was right. Moses could never have lifted the burden alone. God tapped him on the shoulder and gave him assurance of His presence.

Somewhere in the Garden of Gethsemane Jesus felt the tap on the shoulder. God gave Jesus strength to face the cross. An awareness of this truth caused the psalmist to say, "Yea, though I walk through the valley of the shadow of death, I will fear no evil: for thou art with me; thy rod and thy staff they comfort me" (Psalm 23:4).

Such an experience can be ours. God is constantly tapping us on the shoulder and whispering in our ear, "Do not be afraid. I will stand beside you to guide and help you through this situation."

3. Third, we can hold fast to the knowledge that God is on our side. Once the psalmist cried, ". . . for God is for me" (Psalm 56:9). Let us not become confused at this point. God is always on our side, but we are frequently found playing for the opposing team. Our task is to make sure that we are on God's side. If we accomplish this, we will certainly succeed.

The psalmist asked a question that we ought to entertain when our burdens become heavy, "Who is so great a God as our God?" The psalmist thought about the greatness and goodness of God. He talked about God's power and strength. He reminded us that God is adequate for all our needs. This is something we forget. God is on our side and His strength is sufficient. What else do we need to know? It appears to me that this is sufficient. When a man comes to believe, and anchors his hopes on the following truths, there is no problem he cannot solve, and no burden he cannot bear. First, God believes in me, therefore my situation is not hopeless. Second, God walks with me, therefore I am never alone. Third, God is on my side, therefore I cannot lose.

The difference between spiritual success and failure is not so much how many storms we face, but rather how we face them. The record book is filled with illustrations that reflect the truth of this statement.

Several years ago a friend told me about two people whom we knew during the depression: both were very wealthy; both lost their fortunes. One man went home and took a gun and ended his own life; the other went to the altar of his church and prayed. He asked God to give him the courage to face reality and the wisdom to meet the uncertain days ahead with Christian fortitude. One man took his life during the storm, and the other man found his.

Look at the two men who were crucified with Jesus. One of them turned to Jesus and said, ". . . If thou be Christ, save thyself and us" (Luke 23:39). The thief was saying, "I don't believe you are the

Christ. If you were, you would do something about our situation. You are only pretending." This is a cry that God hears daily.

The other man rebuked his companion, for he saw in his own death a bit of justice. He was ready to confess his sins. "We receive the due reward of our deeds: but this man hath done nothing amiss" (Luke 23:41).

The second man turned to Jesus after rebuking his friend and said, ". . . Lord, remember me when thou comest into thy kingdom" (Luke 23:42). This man knew that his plight could not be changed. He was reaping the harvest of an evil past. Jesus was his only hope.

The Master said unto him, ". . . Verily I say unto thee, to day shalt thou be with me in paradise" (Luke 23:43).

The penitent thief caught a glimpse of an eternal truth as he hung on the cross. I think this man must have had a good mother. She surely must have taught him that God does not change. He knew this eternal truth: Pain and sorrow can never obstruct God's love and concern for us. He also knew that man must pay for his sins. He recognized in Christ the only person who could redeem his past. He did not ask to have his immediate situation changed; he merely wanted the courage to face the descending clouds of pain and death. This he could face if God would forgive his sins.

Job knew that God never deserts His people. Job refused to distrust God during his days of darkness. We need to learn this truth. There is no reason to doubt God during moments of sorrow or days of struggle when heavy burdens bear down upon us. God is still God, no matter what happens.

Paul labored in the face of overwhelming opposition. He wrote, "We are troubled on every side, yet not distressed; we are perplexed, but not in despair; persecuted, but not forsaken; cast down, but not destroyed" (II Corinthians 4:8-9). Paul faced prison, shipwrecks, and beatings, not asking God *why*, but thanking Him for the privilege of suffering with Him.

Heavy burdens may try our strength, but they need not weaken us; they may cause us pain, but they need not distress us; they may rest heavy upon our hearts, but they need not crush us. The question that remains is this: "How shall we react to the burdens of life?" Let me suggest five things to remember when the burdens of life press upon us.

38

1. We must learn to accept our burdens as a part of life. The burdens of life, as well as the joys of life, represent a part of the price we must pay for the privilege of living. The quicker we come to recognize this truth the more victorious we shall be in dealing with life's perplexities. Someone has written:

> We are not here to play, to dream and drift,
> We have work to do and loads to lift,
> Shun not the struggle, face it, 'tis God's gift.

Job came to the conclusion that trials are a part of life. "Yet man is born unto trouble," said Job, "as the sparks fly upward" (Job 5:7). That is to say, we cannot avoid the tribulations of life, therefore, we must accept them.

For many weeks, I visited a man who was in great pain; naturally, he was depressed. The doctors had not been able to find the cause of his pain. One day he seemed better, and I asked him if the cause of his suffering had been found.

"Yes," he replied, "the cause has been found, and there is nothing that can be done to help me. The doctor told me the diagnosis, and after he left I asked God to give me the grace to accept this as a part of my life. He has already given me that strength." When a man learns to accept the things that life brings which cannot be changed, he is well on the road to overcoming his burdens.

2. We ought to make up our minds to be faithful. You do not become a competent doctor, an effective preacher, or a good parent by accident. You have to work at it. The people who succeed are the folks who make up their minds to succeed. "I have found," wrote Lincoln, "that most people are about as happy as they make up their minds to be."

To be completely faithful is not as easy as it sounds. Suppose a young high-school student hears the call of God to enter the ministry to become a missionary to some foreign land. Then, suppose the student makes up his mind to respond. The decision is only the first step; there are many years of preparation. He must go to college and attend a theological school. He will be required to study the language of the people with whom he will live and serve. All this requires determination, discipline, and effort.

39

Moses warned Israel about the temptations they would encounter in the strange lands through which they would pass. He tried to prepare them for the difficult journey. In days of tribulation if you seek God, you will surely find Him. Moses assured the Hebrews that this is the only door of hope that would always be open to them. When tribulations are upon you, ". . . turn to the Lord thy God, . . ." said Moses, "For the Lord thy God is a merciful God; he will not forsake thee . . ." (Deuteronomy 4:30-31). When we make up our minds and submit ourselves to God, no burden is unbearable.

Just before his death, Joshua called the tribes of Israel together and talked to them. Joshua challenged the people to make up their minds about whom they would serve. Pagan gods had attracted them at times. In Joshua's valedictory he reminded the children of God's goodness and urged them to choose whom they would serve. Then, Joshua told the people that he had made up his mind; ". . . We will serve the Lord" (Joshua 24:15).

I know a man who at one time in his life had just about become a slave to alcohol. He soon discovered that he was losing his family and that alcohol was ruining his health. One day he made a covenant with God to stop drinking. "I'll furnish the effort," he told God, "if you'll furnish the strength." He had made up his mind to stop drinking. This was the first step, and for week after week he struggled. It was a tremendous battle, but God kept His end of the bargain. One day the man failed to put forth the effort and slipped back to the bottle. Again, he promised God he would try if God would help him. He asked God to forgive his sins. The struggle within this man is still going on, but I know God will help him and I believe that together they will win the struggle.

3. Let us grab hold of our hopes and take God as our partner. Mr. R. L. Middleton tells a story about Clarence Powell; there was a time in the life of this man when he found his financial situation most alarming. As a young married man Powell worked with a construction company. He made an adequate salary as long as he worked, but there were periods when the company had no work to be done. The Powells were the parents of six children, and one fall just before school was due to begin, they discovered that three of their children had worn out their shoes. They had worn them out skipping, and using their feet for brakes as they coasted down a hill in their wagons. In the meantime, the family washing machine had broken

down hopelessly and Clarence Powell searched the newspapers in an effort to find a second-hand machine for sale. He found one advertised and went to the address which was listed.

The house was large and beautiful, so much so that Powell was reluctant to enter. When he rang the doorbell, a kind-looking gentleman answered. Powell told him that he had come to look at the washing machine and he was invited into the house. As he walked to the kitchen to see the machine, he looked in astonishment. Everything was so convenient and beautiful. The man and his wife offered to sell the machine for such a small amount that Clarence, in an effort to express his gratitude, thanked them kindly and at the same time told them that he was in financial difficulty, explaining that he had no work and three of his children had completely worn out their shoes. As he finished speaking, the lady left the room, sobbing as if her heart would break. "Did I say something wrong?" asked Clarence.

"No," replied the husband, "you didn't say anything wrong. You were talking about children's shoes being worn out. We have only one child, a little girl, and she's never walked a step in her life. A pair of worn-out shoes would make us very happy."

After this experience Clarence Powell said, "I went back home and went up to my room and closed the door. I got down on my knees and asked the Lord to forgive me for fretting about little things. I got those three pairs of shoes and looked at them and smiled. I was so thankful for three pairs of worn-out shoes. . . ." We would forget some of our burdens if we focused our attention on the many good things we enjoy from God instead of brooding over our burdens.

When David received word that "the hearts of the people of Israel are after Absalom," he placed his life in the hands of God and said, ". . . let him do to me as seemeth good unto him" (II Samuel 15:26). Instead of spending our energy rebelling against God, we should seek His will and in this search we shall find His peace.

4. We should resolve to live each day to the best of our ability. I am convinced that marriages break up, men fail in business, and people fall under the weight of pressing cares, all because we do not practice what we know is best. Men do not fail because of lack of knowledge: They fail because they do not do the things they know they ought to do in their daily lives.

The prophet proclaimed a long time ago that we know the rules of life; ". . . and what doth the Lord require of thee, but to do justly, and to love mercy, and to walk humbly with thy God?" (Micah 6:8).

I frequently give people two bits of advice; I believe it is good medicine. Most of us need this advice. First, do your best. Let each of us search his heart and ask himself the question, "Am I doing my best to make life what it ought to be?" Most of us would have to answer *no*. Then, I advise many people to slow down. We do our best work when we take time out and give all our talents and energies to the task at hand. The only animal that can do its work more efficiently while in a hurry is a race horse.

Carlyle, in one of his essays, wrote, "You should not worry about the dim, unknown and unknowable future, but you should view the duty that is closest at hand and accomplish as best you can the task that needs to be done this day." It was Jesus who said, "Take therefore no thought for the morrow: for the morrow shall take thought for the things of itself . . ." (Matthew 6:34). Jesus also taught His disciples to pray, "Give us this day our daily bread."

"It has been well said," remarked George Macdonald, "that no man ever sank under the burden of the day. It is when tomorrow's burden is added to the burden of today that the weight is more than a man can bear. Never load yourselves so, my friends. If you find yourselves so loaded, at least remember this: it is your own doing, not God's. He begs you to leave the future to Him and mind the present." Take one step at a time. Remember that "the longest journey begins with a single step."

5. Finally, let us cast our burdens upon the Lord. The psalmist wrote, several hundred years ago: "Cast thy burden upon the Lord, and he shall sustain thee . . ." (Psalm 55:22). This means that we can be sustained. Most of us look for bargains in life and here is a bargain that we can't afford to miss. God will provide the strength, and we furnish the burdens. God promised the children of Israel that they would be equal to the burdens they might encounter on the long journey through the wilderness. ". . . as thy days, so shall thy strength be" (Deuteronomy 33:25). Surely this means no less than to place our burdens upon the strong shoulders of God and He will help us bear them.

Iona Henry lost her fourteen-year-old daughter Jane, with a

brain tumor. A month later Iona Henry, her husband Pete, and Jack, their ten-year-old son, decided to visit Pete's father. They began the journey early one morning. On the third day of the trip they met tragedy. A fast-moving freight train hit their car as they attempted to cross the railroad track near St. Louis. Pete and Jack were killed instantly, and Iona Henry was critically injured. Would Iona Henry live? This was the big question that trained doctors and nurses could not answer. If she knew that her son and husband were dead, would she want to live? Could she find the strength and courage to pick up the broken dreams of life and make out of them a new life? Would she be able to find in her sorrow a purpose that would challenge her? Only time would tell; these were questions that she would have to answer for herself. Many weeks passed, and then months; the struggle was on. It was not between God and Iona Henry. God loved her; she belonged to Him. He was standing by to help her. The struggle was between Iona Henry and God. It was her move. How would she react?

There were lonely days when Iona felt alone. Her mind and heart became a great battlefield. Iona won; she cast her burden upon the Lord, and the Lord lived up to His promise. He sustained her. This is the answer Iona Henry heard from God; she tells it in her own words. God said, "Iona Henry, put your hand in the hand of the God you know is there. Stop insisting that you will do what you want to do, like a spoiled, sulking child, and do what you must do. What must be done may seem impossible, but God has a way of working out the impossible." Under the weight of a broken body and the loss of her entire family, Iona Henry found the strength and presence of God sufficient. God built a bridge to span the vast chasm of sorrow over which she walked to a new life.

When she had received this word from God, Iona Henry said, "A strange new peace and relaxation flooded over me such as I had not known since the fearful trial began. . . . The little questions turned and ran; they were not important any more. The tension went out of me; the strain eased. I was completely relaxed."

Let us take our burdens trustingly to the Father. He will either remove them or give us courage to bear them. It was Jesus who said, "Come unto me, all ye that labour and are heavy laden, and I will give you rest" (Matthew 11:28). Do you believe that? I do.

43

3 TROUBLE:
God, the Light Eternal

ONE OF THE greatest lessons one can learn in the schoolroom of life is how to face trouble successfully. One very fine definition of trouble is this: "Trouble is that which disturbs or agitates us mentally or spiritually." Trouble finds its way into the millionaire's mansion as well as the peasant's hut. It comes to the intellectual giant as well as the illiterate. It visits the saint and the sinner alike. No man travels the road of life without passing through the dark tunnels of trouble.

Trouble travels in many costumes. Frequently it comes wearing strange garments: some persons have mental troubles; others know physical trouble; still others are faced with spiritual troubles.

Since all trouble is not alike, it stands to reason that the springs from which trouble flows are many. For example, none could intelligently deny that we ourselves are the cause of many of our heartaches. I talked with a man once who was being discharged from his position. He was a junior executive and had been very successful. One day one of his superiors discovered several thousand dollars missing. The auditors could not find a record of expenditure to account for the money; the man finally and regretfully confessed that he had stolen it. The man explained that he had become involved in gambling and had lost his savings and decided to take some of the company's money to win back his losses; he had every intention of paying the money back to the company; however, not only did he fail to win, he lost the money he had taken, and as a

44

result could not repay it. "My life is in a mess," he said, "and I know that I am responsible for the troubles I am facing." It is clearly evident that much of our trouble is a result of our own stubbornness, stupidity, and selfishness.

Others bring trouble upon us, and we are frequently responsible for the trouble others bear. I know a man who has been a source of constant worry to his parents. He left school when he was in the eighth grade, and he is habitually in trouble with the civil authorities. He has already served one term in prison. The casual observer would recognize that by this man's determination to satisfy his evil desires and his flagrant disregard for the rights and feelings of others, he has placed a bag full of trouble upon the shoulders of his parents.

In addition, there are unannounced troubles that come unexpectedly. They seem to come from beyond the realm of human activity. We cannot discover a motivating force behind them. With all our intelligence and wisdom, try as we may, we cannot evade them. We, therefore, must come to the conclusion that some troubles must be faced.

My telephone rang late one night and on the line was a nurse calling from one of the large hospitals in my city. "We have a patient here who would like to see you. The doctor tried to reach you earlier. The patient will undergo major surgery in the morning. Can you come tonight?" I told the young lady that I would be there within thirty minutes. It was almost midnight when I arrived on the hospital floor and the nurse took me quietly and quickly toward the patient's room. On the way down the hall she said, "You may call the surgeon if you like, and he will bring you up to date; the only thing I can tell you is that this gentleman is critically ill." She opened the door of the room and whispered, "Stay as long as you like."

I found in that room a man whom I had known and loved for a long time. He twisted the sheet and tossed nervously on the bed. "I apologize for getting you out so late," he said, "but I cannot go into that operating room feeling as I do. I had to talk with you," he continued.

We talked for a long time and then we prayed together. Something strange and marvelous happened. The look of anxiety and fear left

45

the man's face. In its place one could see confidence, serenity, and assurance. I knew he would be able to face the sunrise with an unfaltering trust in the goodness of God. He was no longer restless. When I stood up to leave, he said, "I want to thank you for coming. You will never know how much you have meant to me. I am not afraid any more."

My visit did not change the circumstances; the man was still critically ill. He knew the days ahead would bring suffering and perhaps death. The thing that happened to him could be experienced by every living person. God became real to him. He surrendered his life to God. As soon as he placed his life in the hands of God, he had a different attitude toward his trouble. God took the burdens he could not bear himself; he knew that God was his refuge and strength. With God's help he discovered that he could face life and even death with a song of faith in his heart that enabled him to say with the psalmist, "The Lord is my light and my salvation; whom shall I fear? The Lord is the strength of my life; of whom shall I be afraid?" (Psalm 27:1).

Sometimes trouble weaves a confusing web. It offers no clue to a pattern. Things happen to us that do not make sense. With all our theology and wisdom we find ourselves completely perplexed when we try to take the pieces of trouble and make out of them a logical and sensible picture. During days of trouble I have seen people cry out in utter despair, "Where is God? Why doesn't God do something? Why did this happen to me?" As a pastor I have had to tell people that there is no pat answer to much of the tragedy we experience in life. In spite of this, we must believe that life is good.

One of the finest young couples I know have an afflicted boy. His body is well developed; he looks like a little angel; but he is mentally retarded. There are times when he does not recognize his mother and father, yet they love and care for him with all the tenderness and gentleness of which they are capable. They have a fine Christian spirit toward God. They refuse to be bitter. They have been able, with God's help, to accept their son's handicap with an unwavering faith in the goodness of God.

Some of our troubles do not make sense. An unknown author expressed this truth in the following lines:

46

Not till the loom is silent
And the shuttles cease to fly,
Shall God unroll the canvas
And explain the reason why
The dark threads are as needful
In the weaver's skillful hand
As the threads of gold and silver
In the pattern He has planned.

Jesus expressed one of the deepest thoughts of His heart when He said: "Now is my soul troubled . . ." (John 12:27). The shadow of a cruel cross erected by a ruthless humanity had fallen across the mind of our Lord. Here we see Him in the arena of struggle. It displays His humanity as much if not more than any other record we have regarding our Lord.

The fact that Jesus was troubled does not reflect a divine weakness; rather, it expressed His likeness to you and me. Here we get a glimpse of our Lord behind the curtain, before He marches out on the stage. This is the battleground for the shining victory we see as Jesus hangs on the cross. As Jesus faced this frustrating hour He asked: "And what shall I say? Father, save me from this hour?" That is the cry that often comes from the hearts of men. We do not like to bear burdens or face trouble. "God take us around this experience," we say. Jesus did not linger with this thought. He could see His divine mission mirrored in the cross. "No," He said, "for this purpose I have come to this hour. Father, glorify thy name" (see John 12:27).

In the book, *Days of Our Years*, Pierre van Paassen tells about his sixteenth birthday when his Uncle Kees escorted him upstairs and handed him a set of keys which would open a mysterious black-painted set of bookcases. His old uncle ran his fingers across the back of the books and said, "Here are the lamps that never go out."

God is one of the lamps that will never go out. Jesus walked in the light of that lamp that will never flicker even in the darkest night. When Jesus saw the ugly cross, the lamp seemed to burn brighter. It gave forth its radiant light by which Jesus could walk unfalteringly to His death.

I tell people who face trouble that they can walk in the rays of the eternal light and say with the psalmist, "Thou hast enlarged my steps under me, that my feet did not slip" (Psalm 18:36). We should make every effort to avoid trouble, but at the same time we must concede that there is no detour around many troubles; they are inevitable. Like Jesus, if we are to live successfully, we must face troubles with unquenchable courage.

Ernest Fremont Tittle tells the story of a young man who received a spinal injury during World War II. The doctors told him that he would never walk again. Since the dreadful days of 1944 he has been paralyzed from his waist down. In spite of this tragedy he has learned how to be grateful and happy. He has been able to make a go of life by praying this prayer of St. Francis of Assisi each day: "Grant me the serenity to accept the things I cannot change, courage to change the things I can, and wisdom to know the difference." This is a wise prayer. If circumstances cannot be altered, we have no alternative but to face them with courage if life is to be worthwhile.

I want to suggest six things that we would do well to remember while we are walking under the black shadow of trouble. Perhaps from these suggestions we can find some light that will guide us safely through the storm to the safety of God's harbor.

1. Do not be afraid to face trouble. It is impossible to solve any problem if we are afraid. Jesus was constantly telling people not to be afraid. He knew that we cannot do our best work if fear fills our minds. Jesus did not ignore His troubled mind; He was not afraid to face it. He examined it and decided on a course of action.

When Arthur J. Gossip's wife died, he was left with an emptiness people know only when they lose someone very dear to them. Dr. Gossip was sustained during those days of sorrow by his dauntless faith. On the first Sunday that he mounted the pulpit to preach to his congregation after his wife's death, he spoke with reassuring authority: "I do not think you need to be afraid of life. Our hearts are very frail and there are places where the road is very steep and very lonely, but we have a wonderful God."

The man who believes in the integrity and power of God and repeats as his daily litany the words of the psalmist: "The Lord reigneth; let the earth rejoice . . ." (Psalm 97:1), will never be afraid to face his troubles.

2. Remember that God has created a universe in which He permits trouble. This is not to say that God is the instigator of the

trouble we know, but it is conceivable that God would send us trouble in order for us to achieve a higher good. Now, according to our interpretation, some experiences that help us achieve a higher good might be called trouble, but in God's view they would be called something else.

Christianity does not solve for us the problem of suffering and trouble. On the contrary, it accentuates the problem and makes the solution difficult to find. For example, to join the church and live a righteous life will not make us immune from trouble. Jesus lived the will of God to perfection, yet, at the end of His brief life, He found a cruel cross. If righteous living assures one of a life without sorrow, suffering, and disappointment, Jesus would have experienced endless joy without as much as a single trouble.

3. Remember that God is in our troubles. Again we cannot contend that God is responsible for our troubles; however, I am sure that God is in them. James Stewart writes, "God is not outside the tears and tragedy of life. In every dark valley of trouble and suffering, God is always present." Some people seem to think that God is outside the battleground of human struggle. More than we realize it, God is in the midst of the struggle, commanding His forces.

Benjamin Franklin once said, "I have lived a long time; and the longer I live, the more convincing proofs I see of this truth, that God governs in the affairs of men."

It is difficult, sometimes, to discover God in our troubles. For the disciples, it was next to impossible to see God in the cross. They could see almost everything else in it but God. It was cruel; it was ruthless; it was flagrant injustice. How could God be a part of this? The disciples must have said to themselves, "Certainly, God is not in this ugly picture." But we know that God was there. He was hidden to the disciples by their sorrow and self-pity. Despair covered their souls and all they could see was defeat. Then, Easter came. Standing on this side of Easter, one is likely to forget about the savagery that attended the crucifixion. The victory of Easter overshadows the suffering and shame of the cross. It was not until the first day of the week that the disciples realized that God had been in the cross and had transformed it into an eternal spring from which flows God's mercy and forgiveness.

When I was a boy at home, we sang an old song that has more

meaning for me now than it did then. There is a lot of truth in the words of this song:

> Farther along we'll know more about it,
> Farther along we'll understand why,
> Cheer up, my brother, live in the sunshine,
> We'll understand it all by and by.

Job could not make sense out of his trouble; it just simply did not add up. The Bible tells us that Job was a "perfect and upright" man. He had a large family of seven sons and three daughters. He was also a very rich man. Job lost his wealth, his loved ones, and his body was covered with boils; yet in all of this he managed to express his profound belief that God was in his troubles. "Though he slay me, yet will I trust in him . . ." (Job 13:15).

4. We should be grateful to know that God will supply the strength we need to face life cheerfully during periods of trouble. We read in the Psalms, ". . . call upon me in the day of trouble; I will deliver thee, and thou shalt glorify me" (Psalm 50:15).

I talked with a very sick man recently and asked him to pray with me about his condition. "I don't believe it would do any good for me to call upon God. I am in a tight place now and He probably would not hear me." I told him it was never too late to ask God for strength to bear the load. I reminded him that others have prayed during days of trouble and God heard them. The psalmist said, "I called upon the Lord in distress: the Lord answered me . . ." (Psalm 118:5).

Have you ever come to the place in life where your troubles seemed so much greater than your strength that you felt you had no place to turn? I have seen a great many people face this dilemma. When Jesus became aware of the cross, He was troubled; I suppose many questions came to His mind: Will I have the strength to face the cross and be true to My Father? If the cross cannot be avoided, will God help Me face it? These questions did not tarry long in the mind of Jesus; He regained His poise and knew beyond any doubt that God would give Him the strength to stand unflinchingly before the cross.

There is one thing that I always try to remember about trouble. If there is no way around it, God provides a way through it. If one door is closed, God opens another for us. We all need to know that God will not let us down. We are not always dependable, but God's power is available to us. The psalmist said, ". . . the Lord is the strength of my life; of whom shall I be afraid?" (Psalm 27:1).

Paul talks about his "thorn in the flesh." No one knows exactly what Paul was talking about, but all the scholars agree that it troubled Paul. He prayed about it. He asked God to remove it three times. God did not take this "thorn in the flesh" away. But He did tell Paul this: ". . . My grace is sufficient for thee: for my strength is made perfect in weakness . . ." (II Corinthians 12:9).

Paul was shipwrecked, cast into prison, and beaten many times. Some would have given up, but Paul never retreated. He wrote to Timothy and told him that during the hardships he had endured ". . . the Lord stood with me, and strengthened me . . ." (II Timothy 4:17).

Once there were three Hebrew men who believed in the power of God so strongly that they defied the commands of a pagan king. Nebuchadnezzar, the king of Babylon, ordered all people to bow down when they heard the sound of music and worship a golden image which he had erected. Shadrach, Meshach, and Abednego refused to worship the pagan gods, and the king ordered them to be thrown into the fiery furnace. The Hebrews were not afraid. ". . . our God," they said, "whom we serve is able to deliver us from the burning fiery furnace . . ." (Daniel 3:17). In other words, these men were saying, "God is able to save us from the evil temptation. He could even deliver us from the furnace. Therefore, we are not afraid." They also faced the possibility that God would not deem it wise to save them. What if they should be called upon to die for the faith? "But if not," said these courageous men, "be it known unto thee, O king, that we will not serve thy gods, nor worship the golden image which thou hast set up" (Daniel 3:18). The three men firmly believed that God would give them the strength to remain faithful in temptation and even in death. When you face some overpowering trouble, remember the words of the Hebrews, ". . . our God is able . . ." (Daniel 3:17).

My wife's father owns a beautiful farm in the mountains of north Georgia. Near the house there is a huge spring, where water gushes out of the ground. It is fresh, cool, and pure. The family carry water from the spring to the house in buckets, and the buckets are emptied many times each day. They must be refilled each time. Now these buckets are not sufficient unto themselves. They are simply instruments in which the water is transported. In a sense, you and I are like the buckets. We are not strong enough to bear all the troubles of life alone. We must return frequently to the eternal spring where God's source of strength continually flows. No trouble is too big for God. If we dip our buckets deep into the endless spring of God's power, we can face all our troubles with confidence.

5. Remember that God can use our troubles for our own good as well as for the good of others. The psalmist said, "It is good for me that I have been afflicted . . ." (Psalm 119:71). You will note that I said God can use our troubles; it does not always happen this way. I know a woman who lost her husband unexpectedly; he went to the office one day to work, and was dead before lunchtime. This experience turned the woman against God; she became sullen and bitter. She stopped attending church and lost her faith in God. I know another woman who lost her husband in a tragic automobile accident. She did not take a great interest in church work before this happened, she told me. Now she is found in her pew every time there is a worship service; this tragedy turned her to God. She is gentle, kind, and thoughtful to everyone she meets on the road of life.

Once a lovely lady lost her only son. He was about five years of age. Life, for her, was empty and lonely. In her sorrow, she looked to God for help. God gave her strength to bear her sorrow and faith to carry on. Today, she is a great inspiration to others who face a similar experience. Whenever she hears of a mother who has lost a child, she writes to her with encouraging words. These words are some that she might write: "I know something about the sorrow you feel and the loneliness your heart knows. I, too, lost my only child. He was just a lad. I have found strength to lift my heavy burden and live again. Only God can give you that kind of strength and courage. He has helped me, and I know He will help you. I will be praying for you." Many people have been inspired by this woman's faith. She walked in the darkest night, and found light for living.

Paul wrote, ". . . all things work together for good . . . ," and this is where many people end the quotation. Paul said more than this; he knew that all things do not work together for good. There is too much evil in the world for such a statement to be true. There are too many broken hearts and too much sorrow for us to believe such words. Paul continued, ". . . all things work together for good to them that love God . . ." (Romans 8:28). That little phrase, "to them that love God," makes the difference. I believe Paul was saying that if we love God and remain faithful to Him, He can use our troubles to glorify His name.

Katherine Mansfield let God use her suffering. Before she died, she wrote: "I do not want to die without leaving a record of my belief that suffering can be overcome. For I do believe it. Everything in life that we really accept undergoes a change. So suffering becomes love." Her tender and Christian spirit ripped off the tear-stained garments from the monster of trouble and revealed unto us the noble virtues that God can produce if we give Him a chance to use our troubles.

George MacDonald, in one of his books, wrote about a woman who had experienced a sudden tragedy. The heartache was so crushing and her sorrow so bitter that she spoke aloud, "I wish I'd never been made." Her friend, in what appears to be divine wisdom, whispered, "My dear, you are not made yet. You're only being made and this is the Maker's process." This is but another expression of how we can let God take our troubles and make out of them a garment of Christian fortitude which will not only warm our souls, but will serve to inspire others.

God took Paul, with his disappointments, thorn in the flesh, and opposition, and made out of him a champion of the faith. God took the ugly cross and transformed it into a flowing stream of mercy and forgiveness. I am convinced that God can take each of us with our fears and troubles and make out of us a faithful and worthy disciple.

6. We should always remember that we are never alone. Jesus said to His disciples, ". . . I am with you alway, even unto the end of the world" (Matthew 28:20). It is true that we can never drift out of the channel of God's love and concern. His help is always accessible. He is near to guide us through all the valleys of uncertainty.

I am expressing a well-known truth when I say, "God is with me alway." But God does not help me unless I give Him a chance. I must do my part and ask Him to guide me during periods of trouble.

53

"For I am persuaded, that neither death, nor life, nor angels, nor principalities, nor powers, nor things present, nor things to come, nor height, nor depth, nor any other creature, shall be able to separate us from the love of God, which is in Christ Jesus our Lord" (Romans 8:38-39). This is what Paul wrote to the church at Rome.

David Livingstone gave his life to a people whose language was strange to him and whose attitude toward him was always uncertain. He never retreated: he died on duty. Before his death Livingstone said the thing that sustained him as he went into one hostile group after another was the knowledge that God was with him. He was constantly among strangers, but he never felt alone.

It is truly a source of courage to discover that we are not alone in our troubles. God stands with us. The psalmist was not afraid, because he knew God was near. "Yea, though I walk through the valley of the shadow of death, I will fear no evil: for thou art with me . . ." (Psalm 23:4).

Epictetus, the Greek stoic philosopher, said, "When you have shut the doors and made a darkness within, remember never to say that you are alone, for you are not alone, God is within."

The cross loomed before Jesus with unprecedented clarity as He prayed in the Garden of Gethsemane. He knew the rest of the journey would be difficult. He left the garden with a resolute heart. Jesus had gained the assurance that the cross would not be an obstacle too big for Him. "God," Jesus must have thought, "will be glorified in the cross." Jesus knew that He was not alone as He trudged to Calvary under the heavy burden of the cross.

As Jesus approached the final days of His earthly life He said to His disciples, "Behold, the hour . . . is now come, that ye shall be scattered, . . . and shall leave me alone: and yet I am not alone, because the Father is with me" (John 16:32).

I have heard the late Dr. W. E. Sangster tell about the terrible days of World War II. Dr. Sangster was minister of Westminster Central Hall in London during those dark days in world history.

One day I was having lunch with Dr. Sangster and he told me that during five long years of the war he never slept once in his own bed; he was busy day and night serving others. In spite of this, he never missed preaching a single Sunday in his church. He said, "For many months I did not have time to prepare a sermon, but when I mounted the pulpit to preach, God was there with me, and He always gave me a message."

Louise Haskins, in "The Gate of the Year," wrote,

And I said to the man who stood at the gate of the year:
"Give me a light, that I may tread safely into the unknown!"
And he replied:
"Go out into the darkness and put your hand into the Hand of God.
That shall be to you better than light and safer than a known way."

We are never alone in our troubles. God is always with us. He is able to help us. It seems to me that such knowledge is sufficient for us to live all of life with confidence.

4 DEATH:

Live Life With God;
Face Death Without Fear

CHURCHES EVERYWHERE ARE thronged on Easter Sunday. I dare not say that these masses of people wish only to parade in their Easter finery. Underneath the lovely clothes, buried deep within the soul, there lurk sincere longings. Through the ages, from the first Easter to the present day, man has hailed the message of the risen Christ, and has thrilled anew to the story of the resurrection. In contrast, in the innermost sanctum of his mind, man has pondered the fact of death, and longed for the answer to the many questions which plague his thoughts concerning death—his, and the deaths of those whom he loves.

Most of us have stood beside an open grave to bid farewell to some loved one or close friend. When this earthly pilgrimage is over and when those we love set sail upon that silent sea of death, there emerge within the soul many questions regarding the destiny of man. These longings of the heart cry out for the answer to the eternal question concerning what happens to man at the end of his earthly journey, as a thirsty man cries out for a cool drink of water to ease the discomfort of a parched tongue.

Those of us who stand upon the sandy shores of earthly life look with eager hearts upon the mighty ocean of death. If, with human eyes, we could see the other shore, we could go about our business with peaceful hearts; but the expanse is too wide. We cannot see the other side with human eyes. How happy we would be if we were assured that those we love have anchored their little ships in God's eternal harbor.

I have seen men, after they have mustered up all the hope and courage at their command, permit doubts to flood their minds, fear to capture their powers of reason, and despair to capture their hopes. These enemies of Christian faith have, at times, pushed the devoted and faithful disciples into a room temporarily filled with suspicion and doubt about life after death.

I would be less than intelligent if I were to assume that on the following pages I could convince the atheist, agnostic, or cynic that life is eternal. It appears to me that any intelligent view of the universe, the nature of man, and the reality of God would lead one to recognize the necessity for belief in immortality. We are learning more and more about the orderliness of the universe. The harmony of planets as well as a learned explanation of our surroundings tell us that some intelligent Creator must be behind this creative activity.

The most reasonable explanation of human life points to immortality. There are some obstacles to overcome to reach this conclusion, but the alternatives present mountain after mountain of perplexing problems which cannot be solved.

Immortality is more than a product of man's wishful thinking. It is a divine reality. It is not a soothing tonic that we take to camouflage death and to comfort with a brave illusion the broken heart; it is as much a fact as life itself.

The average person finds it difficult to break away from the common experience of judging the reality of a thing by the standard of the five senses. We place a lot of importance on the appearance of things. We believe more quickly the things we are able to see and touch. Conversely, we find it difficult to believe in the things beyond our limited world of experience with the five senses.

Here is the major problem in accepting, without any doubt, eternal life. All our experiences speak against it. We have never been permitted to look beyond the grave. We have seen no traveler who has returned from the unknown land which we call death; death looks like the end. Our loved ones, whom we have known in the flesh, are limp and lifeless. They cannot speak. There is no evidence of survival.

To doubt life after death because there seems to be no outward appearance to support this fact is actually unscientific. If science has taught us one thing about the world around us, it is that the outward appearance of a thing is deceiving. You cannot depend upon your five senses to reveal the reality of a thing.

My family and I live in a lovely brick house. It looks secure and solid. I have no fear of its collapsing. Every brick is in its place; yet the fact remains, according to scientific truth, that every brick in my house is a moving mass of electrons. Therefore, as this one instance shows, it is a scientific fact that we cannot ascertain the reality of a thing by its appearance.

Sir Arthur Eddington, the English astronomer, wrote, "We are no longer tempted to condemn the spiritual aspects of our nature as illusory because of their lack of concreteness. We have traveled far from the standpoint which identifies the real with the concrete." The greatest part of life and the things that make life real are composed of that vast store of intangibles. Character is invisible, yet it marches in the army of reality. Love is not as concrete as a cookstove, but no intelligent person would deny its reality. Truth cannot be seen, yet we know that truth exists. Death may look final, but this is only an illusion. In reality, death is only the elevator that takes us to a higher floor in the building of life.

Harry Emerson Fosdick has reminded us, ". . . that unless Germany denies that men like Kant are her deep-seeing prophets; unless England chooses lesser souls than her Wordsworth, Browning and Tennyson to represent her loftiest spiritual insight; unless America says to Emerson, Whittier and to their like that they are not our seers; man must confess that with marvelous unanimity the most elevated and far-seeing spirits of the race have most believed in immortality."

Every Sunday millions say, "I believe in the resurrection." Do we really mean this? Is it something we say glibly without any real meaning? Men of all ages have asked, "If a man die, shall he live again?" That agonizing question raises its head when we stand by the open grave with a feeling of irreparable loss and it disturbs our faith. Unless Jesus was a hoax, a sneaky imposter, a designed cheat, and a deceiving liar, He gave us the true answer when He said, "I am the resurrection, and the life; he that believeth in me, though

58

he were dead, yet shall he live. And whosoever liveth and believeth in me shall never die . . ." (John 11:25-26).

Can we believe these words of Jesus? The answer is "Yes." When these words are written upon the heart, we can march to the sunset of life, not with sad words of parting upon our lips, but with a triumphant song of Easter in our hearts.

The greatest message God ever sent to the world was spelled out upon the cross. It tells us of a love that is unfathomable and which defies description. The cross was only a part of the message.

The Cathedral of Winchester in England holds a story that has become tradition; it tells of how the news of the Battle of Waterloo was first received in London. The news came to the south coast by ship, and was sent on to London by signals. As the message reached Winchester it was spelled out by signals, "W-E-L-L-I-N-G-T-O-N D-E-F-E-A-T-E-D . . . ," and then the fog rolled in and the signals were no longer visible. The news of supposed defeat spread quickly. The whole country was saddened by the message, which actually was incomplete; yet it looked final. When the fog lifted, the signals on Winchester Cathedral were busy spelling out the complete message: it read, "WELLINGTON DEFEATED THE ENEMY." This news changed the picture. It changed the situation from defeat to victory and from gloom to gladness.

God finished His message to humanity three days after Calvary. On Easter morning the friends of Jesus found the tomb empty. Their lives of gloom were changed immediately to happiness. At a casual glance the message of the cross looks like defeat, but this is only a part of the message. Death also looks like the end; but I believe Easter morning gave us the only answer we need to know to assure us that beyond the gate of death is a land filled with the living. The Christian church has conclusive evidence that men live after death. The claims for eternal life rest squarely upon the resurrection of our Lord. The entire structure of the Christian faith has its foundation on the truth of Easter.

Ralph Turnbull, in his book, *The Pathway to the Cross*, relates the story of a Moslem who approached a Christian with these words, "We Moslems have one thing you Christians do not have."

"What is that?" replied the Christian.

"When we go to Medina," continued the Moslem, "we find a

59

coffin and know that Mohammed lived because his body is in the coffin. But when you Christians go to Jerusalem, you find nothing but an empty tomb."

"Thank you," commented the Christian. "What you say is absolutely true and that makes the eternal difference. We find in Jerusalem an empty tomb because our Lord lives and we serve a risen Christ."

The critics have failed to explain away the fact of the resurrection. Every effort has failed. Let me hurriedly suggest some of the attempts to explain away the fact of the resurrection.

1. Some people say that Jesus was not dead when He was removed from the cross; they maintain that He was only in a state of unconsciousness. The seasoned Roman soldiers knew when their job was finished. They examined the body of Jesus and took a spear and pierced His side until blood and water streamed to the ground. The enemies of Jesus were on hand to see that the execution was completed; they wanted to make certain that He would cause them no more trouble.

When Joseph of Arimathea came to Pilate to request the body of Jesus in order to give Him a decent burial, Pilate marveled that He was dead already. Therefore, he sent word asking the soldier, who was probably in charge of the crucifixion, if Jesus was dead and even inquired as to how long He had been dead. Pilate refused to release the body of Jesus until the soldier assured him that Jesus was dead. He was dead. No student of history would sincerely question that fact.

2. Others have fostered the idea that the chief priests and elders bribed the soldiers who had been stationed at the grave and charged to watch the body for three days to say that they fell asleep, and the disciples stole the body of Jesus. How absurd! If they were asleep, how did they know the disciples took the body? What would the disciples have done with the body? Could the lifeless body of Christ have inspired them to preach and even give their lives for the Kingdom? No one was convinced of the truth of the resurrection more than the disciples.

3. Still others say that the Jews disposed of the body of Jesus. The Jews did not want more trouble than they already had. Yet, when Peter began preaching the resurrection of Christ, they were

disturbed. The Sadducees, the priests and the Captain of the Temple arrested the disciples and held them imprisoned overnight. The next day, Annas, Caiaphas, and the elders and scribes held a council. ". . . What shall we do to these men? for that indeed a notable miracle hath been done by them is manifest to all them that dwell in Jerusalem; and we cannot deny it" (Acts 4:16). They decided to reprimand the disciples and caution them not to mention or teach in the name of Jesus. If they had taken the body of Jesus, they would have revealed this fact in order to clip this new movement in its infancy.

4. Finally, there are those who say the body was buried in a common burial ground, and the women went to the wrong tomb. This is contrary to all available evidence. In the first place, Joseph, a friend of our Lord, buried Him. Then, the Jewish leaders persuaded the authorities to place a guard at the grave. The burial spot was a well-known place and the close friends of Jesus as well as His enemies knew the spot. There could be no mistake about this.

Life at its worst is good, and I believe death will be even better. The eyes of faith will lift the soul above the intellectual confusion that places obstacles in the path of reason regarding life after death. Tennyson wrote, "My own dim life should teach me this, that life shall live forevermore."

We are about as weak as we think we are, but when God holds our hands, we are stronger than we ever dreamed. If someone told Iona Henry at Christmas time, 1951, that the future would bring her untold suffering and sorrow she would not have believed him. Suppose someone had whispered in her ear and said, "Iona, before the spring flowers are in full bloom you will have lost your daughter Jane, your son Jack, and your husband Pete; and you will be flat on your back with indescribable pain." Could a weak human stand so much pain and sorrow? No one whispered that message in Iona's ear, but it happened. She tells the moving story in her book, *Triumph Over Tragedy*. The last sentence in that book reads, "For I have walked far in the valleys of the unknown land, and I have come safely through." Death is like that. I believe when we reach the other side, we will greet those we love by saying, "I have walked through the valley of death. There was no need to doubt or fear. God was there to show me the way and I have come through safely."

61

It is not strange that the disciples made no effort to prove the resurrection of Jesus. This was a fact that needed no additional proof. They knew Jesus had conquered death and their job was to spread the news rather than to explain the details of the event. For them, it did not need an explanation. The joy of the victory overshadowed the question of *how*.

It would seem like an incredible proposition to the disciples to waste an ounce of energy on proving the resurrection. Someone asked William James if he believed in infant baptism. He looked utterly amazed as he replied, "Believe in it. Why, man, I've seen it." It would, therefore, represent the height of foolishness to ask the disciples, "Do you believe that Jesus conquered death?" They would look surprised and respond by saying, "Believe in it. Why, man, I saw it." What other proof do you need in order to believe in it?

The various denominations of the Christian church are out of step at many points regarding theology, ritual, and doctrine. We do not all agree, for example, on the form of baptism or the manner of observing the Sacrament of the Lord's Supper. Yet, when it comes to the resurrection, every denomination of the Christian church falls into step. Here we march by the music of the same drummer. We all proclaim without apology, "Hallelujah, Christ Arose!" This is the basic and fundamental fact of the Christian church.

A little five-year-old boy named Eddie was told that his father had been killed. Eddie loved his father. There must have been, in his home, expressions of Christian love and evidence of Christian faith; for Eddie took his father's Bible to the funeral home and placed it in the casket and was heard to remark, "I know Daddy will want his Bible in heaven." Many questions came to the mind of this lad as he stood before the body of his father: "Will he ever come back? Will my Daddy be in heaven? Is he in the ground? Will I ever see him again?"

I want to say this to Eddie and others who have pondered similar questions about loved ones. "Your Daddy won't ever come back in flesh and blood, but I am convinced that our dead are closer to us than we can ever imagine. Your Daddy is not in the ground. His body, which is only the temple of his soul, is in the ground; but the soul and personality of your Daddy, which are your real Daddy, are safe in the loving hands of God. Oh yes, you will see him again. Somehow, somewhere, by the goodness and grace of God, you'll see him, know him, and love him."

We base our claim for eternal life on the resurrection of our Lord. He lived; He died; and He rose from the dead and lives eternally in the hearts of men and in the presence of God. I believe in the resurrection, and here is why. I believe in the resurrection because apart from it, we cannot account for the Christian church. The birth of the Christian church came out of the belief that Jesus was the long-awaited Messiah. The church was organized around a living Christ, not a dead Messiah. The service of Holy Communion symbolizes both the death of our Lord and His resurrection. Here we testify to His power to forgive sins and fill the future with hope and peace. A dead Christ could not do that.

The fact that the day of worship was changed from the seventh day of the week to the first day of the week is evidence of His resurrection. The traditional sacred day that was set aside for worship was the Sabbath or seventh day of the week. The followers of Christ changed this day when they were certain that Christ rose from the dead.

Unless Jesus conquered the grave, the Christian faith and indeed the Christian church are based upon illusions. After nearly twenty centuries, it scarcely seems possible that this could represent the truth. Sometimes men become the victims of illusions; we measure life by false values. Yet, history clearly shows us that the end is misery and certain death. Illusions let you down; they deceive you. Only the real truth holds you up and brings you to the goal.

The truth of the resurrection and the power of the risen Lord have stood the test of time. They are just as powerful today as they were on Pentecost. Ernest Fremont Tittle has reminded us that where men have really tried and lived by the power of the risen Christ, it has brought new life. "It has lifted men out of despair into hope, out of selfishness, pettiness and meanness into lively concern for others. . . . It has brought forth the idea of a universal brotherhood of man and a vision of a world redeemed from hunger, poverty, chaos, and war. . . ." A church with a heart and conscience such as this cannot be accounted for other than through the risen Lord. This is the only adequate explanation. We need to recognize that the resurrection story did not grow out of the church; rather, the church grew out of the resurrection. The living Lord brings power to the church of this century.

Then, I believe in the resurrection because of the reliable reports of those who saw the risen Lord. The Gospel according to Matthew records two appearances made on earth by Jesus after the resurrection.

As Mary Magdalene and the other Mary approached the tomb early the first day of the week, they were told by an angel that Jesus had conquered the grave. They were instructed to take the news to the eleven disciples. While on the way, ". . . Jesus met them, saying, All hail. And they came and held him by the feet, and worshipped him" (Matthew 28:9).

After the disciples received word that Jesus was alive, they went into Galilee and to a mountain where Jesus had appointed them. It was here, according to Matthew, that the disciples received their first glimpse of the risen Lord. ". . . they saw him, they worshipped him: but some doubted" (Matthew 28:17).

The Gospel of Mark, the oldest of the gospels, mentions several appearances of the risen Lord. However, it is felt by biblical scholars that the last part of the original chapter of Mark was lost. The last twelve verses of the present sixteenth chapter seem to have been written by some later author. However, the resurrection was reported in the section of the last chapter which was a part of the original. It seems probable that the writer of the last verses of Mark was familiar with the original document.

In its present form, Mark's Gospel reports that Jesus made three appearances. First, He appeared to Mary Magdalene (Mark 16:9). Then, ". . . he appeared in another form unto two of them, as they walked, and went into the country" (Mark 16:12). Finally, ". . . he appeared unto the eleven as they sat at meat, and upbraided them with their unbelief and hardness of heart, because they believed not them which had seen him after he had risen" (Mark 16:14).

Luke's Gospel records the risen Lord as having made three appearances. First, Jesus appeared to two disciples on the road to Emmaus. Jesus talked with them as they journeyed and visited with them when they reached their destination. As Jesus broke bread and gave it to them they recognized Him, then He vanished out of their sight. Too, there is a reference indicating that Jesus appeared unto Simon Peter. Finally, He appeared before the eleven disciples and they were invited to touch His body. They talked together and Jesus ". . . did eat before them" (Luke 24:43).

John, in his Gospel, speaks of four appearances made by our Lord. When Mary Magdalene found the tomb empty, she reported this to the disciples. As she stood in the garden weeping, Jesus spoke to her, ". . . why weepest thou? whom seekest thou? She, supposing him to be the gardener, saith unto him, Sir, if thou have borne him hence, tell me where thou hast laid him, and I will take him away. Jesus saith unto her, Mary. She turned herself, and saith unto him, Rabboni, which is to say, Master" (John 20:15-16).

On the same day Jesus appeared unto the disciples; Thomas was absent. The disciples examined Jesus. They knew He was their Lord. Then He appeared to the disciples again and Thomas was present. When Thomas looked upon Jesus, he said, ". . . My Lord and my God" (John 20:28). Finally, John reports that Jesus appeared to seven of the disciples on the shores of Galilee. When Peter heard one of the disciples say, "It is the Lord," he jumped into the sea and made his way toward Jesus.

These chosen few experienced the risen Lord; they reached a new level of joy and gladness as they discovered that Jesus had conquered the grave. I believe in the resurrection because of these reliable reports.

Finally, I believe in the resurrection of our Lord because of the attitude of the disciples and friends of Jesus. One must go back to Calvary in order to get a true picture of the attitude that was common to the friends of our Lord. Despair and hopelessness were written all over the faces of the disciples. Their dreams were crushed, their hopes shattered. They looked at each other with a stare of indescribable emptiness: Jesus was dead, His body was limp. The summer sun sank below the horizon and the shadow of three crosses played on the hillside. The shadow of one cross reached backward to God and it has played across the hearts of men in every century.

The attitude of Peter reflects the feelings of the others. Suppose, in fancy, we travel back across the centuries and talk with Peter. The stage is set. The scene is just after the crucifixion, nineteen

65

centuries ago. The first speaker asks, "Peter, what do you think about the future?"

"Future, you ask," replies Peter. "There is no future without Christ. He was our hope, and now He's dead. Who cares about the future? We fought a losing battle." Peter turns to walk away. "I don't want to talk about it. I am going fishing." That is the prevailing attitude. Doubt, fear, and sheer hopelessness are evident in the lives of the disciples.

The disciples did not expect Jesus to conquer death. This is a strange note, yet, I believe, a true one. Not a single disciple accepted the truth of the resurrection at first without the shadow of doubt covering his mind.

Let us look at the record. According to Matthew's Gospel, when Jesus appeared to the disciples they saw Him and worshiped Him; ". . . but some doubted" (Matthew 28:17). It was a difficult truth to accept, not because they did not want to believe it, but because they lacked faith.

As written in Mark's Gospel, when the disciples heard that Jesus was alive and had been seen by a woman of integrity, they ". . . believed not" (Mark 16:11). Why did these disciples find doubt so easy and faith so scarce? They were like men of this century; when we stand by the grave of one we love, we want to believe, but sometimes it is difficult to believe.

According to the writer of Luke, when the women told the disciples that Jesus had come back to life, the attitude of the disciples was recorded in these words: "And their words seemed to them as idle tales, and they believed them not" (Luke 24:11). Again when Jesus appeared before them, they were terrified with fear and believed that they had seen a spirit.

According to John's account of the resurrection, when Mary Magdalene went to tell the disciples that Jesus was alive, she found them behind locked doors, trembling with fear. This is evidence that they did not expect Jesus to return from the halls of death. Thomas, one of the twelve, refused to believe even after the other disciples, all of whom were honest, told him that they had seen the Lord. Thomas said, ". . . Except I shall see in his hands the print of the nails, and put my finger into the print of the nails, and thrust my hand into his side, I will not believe" (John 20:25).

Finally the disciples accepted the truth of the resurrection. They believed what their hearts wanted to believe because they experienced the power and presence of the living Lord. Their doubts were changed to faith, their despair to joy, their fears to courage, their weakness to strength, and their gloom to assurance.

The disciples came from behind their locked doors. They preached in the streets, for they were no longer afraid of the Jews. They were persecuted and beaten, yet they continued to proclaim their undying faith in the power of the risen Lord. They even died for the faith they preached. Death held no terror for them, for Christ arose from the dead and this was all the assurance they needed. They, too, would live for eternity.

Apart from the complete acceptance of the resurrection of Jesus the attitude of the disciples and friends of Jesus cannot be explained. There is in every soul a divine spark which all the winds of earth and devils of hell cannot extinguish. I believe that life is eternal.

The injustices of earth support my belief in everlasting life. Think of the uncounted thousands of youths from every land who, in battle, have been cut down in the prime of life. There is a vast army of children who have died because of the evils of war. Millions have entered an early grave because of disease, lack of food, and because of accidents, storms, and other tragedies. Think of the millions who live in Asiatic lands for whom life is a constant struggle against poverty and disease; they must struggle even to stay alive. What about the people who live in every land, including our own, who are compelled to live from birth to death in ugly surroundings without hope of an opportunity to enjoy proper food, housing, and clothing?

Mozart promised the world great music; yet the end of his earthly pilgrimage came at thirty-five. Keats wrote beautiful poetry which could calm restless hearts; yet he died at the age of twenty-six. Jesus was in the prime of life; yet He died on the cross at the age of thirty-three.

Surely man is not created simply for the little speck of life he knows here. For many, life is misery; for all of us it is a mixture of joy and sorrow, victory and defeat. God did not make man to cast him on the scrap-pile after a few fleeting years. Death is not the end. Our dreams, for the most part, are unrealized; our aspirations are unfulfilled, and our talents not yet developed.

The character of God supports my belief in life after death.

There are many things that we do not know about God. Yet, we know enough about Him to believe that He loves us. God knows all about us. He cares for us and heals our broken hearts. God is completely honest and trustworthy. The world about us teaches that man is somehow tied to the eternal. God has placed within us a restlessness which cannot be satisfied by anything except the divine. God has placed within us a spark that believes in and longs for life eternal; He will not deny the satisfaction of that spark.

Death, if we can trust the character of God—and I believe we can—is not a dead-end street; it is a passageway to God's eternal throne. James S. Stewart reminds us that "if the great Father has loved His children enough to go into the far country after them, to climb the terrible slopes of Calvary for them, to send the urgency and passion of His Holy Spirit to revive and rescue them, . . . If God so loved the world—do you imagine that He will consent to have His love balked and thwarted and robbed by death at the end of the day?" This endless and unrelenting search for man supports my belief in eternal life.

Then, I believe in eternal life because I see death as a part of God's divine and intelligent plan for man. Our existence follows a natural pattern. We are born, we live for a while, and then we come to the close of our earthly pilgrimage. Someone has rightly said, "This is the world of the dying and the next is the world of the living."

Life is like the day and death is like the sunset. The day, like life, begins in the morning. The hours and minutes tick away until finally, darkness comes; the sun sets; we see it no more. Our loved ones die and we bid them farewell. Yet, those of us who know anything about geography and the nature of the universe know that as the sun sets for us it is shining on another continent and lighting the way for other people. It follows that those of us who look at life through the eyes of Christian faith know that our loved ones are not dead. They are living on another continent, with God and His people.

When we learn to accept death as God's plan, we lose our fear. Death must be good, because all of God's plans for us are good. They are worked out in God's laboratory of wisdom and in the presence of divine love. Jonathan Swift wrote, "It is impossible that anything so natural, so necessary and so universal as death should ever have been designed by Providence as an evil to mankind."

Not too long ago I stood by a hospital bed and looked into the face of a young man who had been the tragic victim of an automobile accident. He was as helpless as a baby, yet at times so violent he had to be tied to his bed. The doctor said he would never be normal again; he had received a severe brain injury and would always be helpless. It was sheer agony for the loved ones of this man to see him in such a condition. Only a few days before, he was a strong healthy young man. Death finally took him. Standing outside the room in the corridor of the hospital, one could almost hear the loved ones say, "Thank God for death." In this case, death was a good friend.

Death does not always appear as one's friend. At times, it looks like a cruel enemy coming to crush our hearts. I remember standing by the grave of a little seven-year-old girl who had died suddenly. Her life was just beginning. It was almost an impossible task to comfort her distraught parents. I was frank to tell them I was baffled and did not pretend to have an answer to the question *why*. "There is one thing I know," I told them, "death is a part of God's plan, and while we do not understand it, I know it is a good plan. God sees life in its entirety, and we see only a few fleeting years. God knows best and we must trust Him in a tragedy such as this, a tragedy so perplexing that all human wisdom cannot hope to give a satisfying answer."

I believe in life eternal because of the teachings of our Lord. When Jesus went to Bethany, where His friend, Lazarus, had died, He was greeted by Martha and Mary. They did not expect Jesus to raise their brother from the dead, but Jesus looked at Martha and said, ". . . I am the resurrection, and the life: he that believeth in me, though he were dead, yet shall he live" (John 11:25). Then Jesus prayed and called Lazarus from the dead.

Jesus tried to prepare His disciples for the events they would experience near the end of His earthly ministry. He told them He would suffer many things and even die, but they should not be troubled. Then He said, ". . . I will come to you. Yet a little while, and the world seeth me no more; but ye see me: because

I live, ye shall live also. At that day ye shall know that I am in my Father, and ye in me, and I in you" (John 14:18, 19).

Death is the experience of going to God rather than a time of ceasing to live. It is a door by which the Christian enters the Father's house, rather than some dead-end street. As some anonymous author has written:

> The tomb is not an endless night,
> It is a thoroughfare, a way,
> That closes in soft twilight,
> And opens in eternal day.

Jesus trusted His Father in death. As He hung on the cross, He knew His life was not over and He kept His serenity and faith even though indescribable pain pierced His body with every heartbeat. Above the noise of the crowd, the darkness was filled with the voice of One who was confident as He cried, ". . . Father, into thy hands I commend my spirit . . ." (Luke 23:46). Jesus was simply saying, "Father, life for Me on earth is over. Now, I am coming home."

Then, I believe in life everlasting because it is a universal belief. Men of every age and circumstance have believed there is some form of life after death. When Michael Faraday, the British chemist and physicist, was on his deathbed someone asked him, "Dr. Faraday, what do you speculate concerning the future?" The old man, with one eye on the earth and the other looking in on heaven, said, "I have been speculating in my laboratory for nearly fifty years; I will no longer deal in the area of speculation. I will deal with certainties from now on." Earth was real to him, but heaven was even more of a reality.

"When I go down to the grave," wrote Victor Hugo, "I can say, like so many others, I have finished my work; but I cannot say I have finished my life. My life will continue. My tomb is not a blind alley. It is a thoroughfare."

Robert Ingersol, the avowed infidel, said at his brother's funeral, "From the voiceless lips of the unreplying dead there comes no word. But in the night of Death, Hope sees a star, and listening Love can hear the rustling of a wing."

William Thackeray wrote, "Life is the soul's nursery—its training place for the destinies of eternity." Henry Wadsworth Longfellow wrote:

> There is no death! What seems so is transition.
> This life of mortal breath
> Is but a suburb of the life elysian,
> Whose portal we call Death.

The final and undebatable evidence of eternal life for me is found within my soul. It is an experience, not a doctrine or a belief. This experience has been born out of a struggle and prayer. I have come to know Jesus as a living Lord and not a dead figure of the past. You might shake my beliefs; you might change doctrine, but you will never be able to destroy this experience.

I belong to God, not only for the few fleeting years we call life, but for eternity. He is on both sides of the river. I am in God's presence in life, in death, and even forever. I like the story that I read many years ago, as told by another minister.

Once a father and his son went mountain-climbing. There were some steep and dangerous places on the path they chose. As they were climbing one of these treacherous places, someone called out to the little boy, "Do you have a good hold on your father, lad?"

The little lad replied, "No, but he has a good hold on me." This exemplifies a significant truth. If I depend upon my grip on the Father for security, I will be likely to stumble and fall. The thing that keeps me going is the knowledge that my Father has a good grip on me. I know that in death He does not loosen His grip.

There are a good many mysteries about death, but I press on with confidence, believing that death is only a graduation from one schoolroom to another, where I shall be ready to begin my advanced studies.

Death is not the final blast on the trumpet of life. It is the prelude to a musical composition that exceeds our most noble hopes and our highest aspirations. Face life with God, and you can face death with undefeatable hope and confidence. Thomas Parnell wrote: "Death's but a path that must be trod—If man would ever pass to God." This, I believe.

5 GRIEF:
Surrender to God

SORROW, GRIEF, AND their companions come to every life. Tennyson wrote, "Never morning wore to evening, but some heart did break." The most difficult thing I have to do as a minister is to pour the refreshing water of comfort upon the hot tears of sorrow. I do not mean that this is distasteful; I find joy in helping people find a rainbow of peace in the dark clouds of sorrow. My heart is crushed and my tongue is almost paralyzed as I stand in the presence of sorrowing souls and broken hearts. Yet when it is my golden opportunity to try to comfort the grief-stricken, I must pray diligently that God will give me the serenity and power to say with convincing sincerity what my heart knows to be true.

Grief can leave the soul desolate and blot out the hopes of the future, or it can draw the soul into the presence of God and enrich life with new dreams and golden hopes never before entertained. The avenue down which the grief-stricken soul will travel depends for its choice upon the ability of the individual to open his heart to the promises and assurances of God.

During my ministry, I have seen grief choke noble aspirations and strangle efforts that would later serve a struggling humanity. Once a man lost his only son with whom he had had a most satisfying relationship. Both the father and his boy seemed to radiate with joy and gladness when they were together. This close relationship was even more pronounced as the boy became a man. One day tragedy struck without warning; the young man was killed instantly. The shock was so great that the father lost all interest in life. He sat in his little world of grief and refused to assume his place of responsibility in a world that needed his talents. He lived only in the past. The future was no longer a challenge or an adventure; it was simply a time to dream about happy memories of a golden past that was gone forever. This man has existed for the last ten years in his secluded room of grief, making absolutely no contribution to the world around him. His life points up the folly of permitting grief to shut out the sunshine of the present, and making the future look dark and hopelessly sad.

In contrast to this man, I have known uncounted dozens of people, both men and women, who have emerged from the valley of grief with a basket full of God's richest blessings. Some respond to sorrow in such a way that it brings them nearer to the heart of God.

I was out in Mississippi preaching a series of services some months ago, and I met a deeply religious man. He gave himself as well as his resources to God's Kingdom in a selfless and generous manner. Every time the doors of the church were open, this man was there. Whenever something needed to be done in the church, he was among the first to volunteer. His sincerity and loyalty impressed me. Before I left, I asked the host pastor about him. His reply was, "He has not always been a good man. There was a time when he ignored God, flouted truth, and looked only to material things for his happiness. He was a very successful man, in material things. Life was a pleasure and he lived in a little selfish world of his own. One day the clouds of trouble darkened his blue sky, and when the storms were over, he had buried his wife and a little girl. That was several years ago, and since then he has been God's man." I like that phrase, "God's man." There is a thrill that cannot be explained about being "God's man or God's woman."

Sometimes it takes a shocking tragedy to cause a person to look up and recognize God and the hopelessness of life without Him. That man in Mississippi walked deep into the chasm of grief. He came out with a true perspective and a high purpose of life. God can take the darkest night and make out of it a temple of praise

73

where one can see in every star the changeless love of a Creator who cares for His people.

Many have walked the road of sorrow and found the truth of the little poem written by Robert B. Hamilton:

> I walked a mile with Pleasure,
>   She chattered all the way,
> But left me none the wiser
>   For all she had to say.

> I walked a mile with Sorrow
>   And ne'er a word said she;
> But, oh, the things I learned from her
>   When Sorrow walked with me!

It is difficult for most people to prepare their hearts in anticipation of grief in such a way that the burden that grief brings does not leave its heavy load of loneliness, despair, and sadness upon the soul. Yet we can, in some measure, analyze grief during our sober moments. An objective analysis of grief will give one some help and guidance in dealing with it when it descends upon him. It is not a question of "Will grief come?" but, rather, "When will it come?"

Grief is inevitable. Man, no matter upon what rung of civilization he finds himself, will one day come face to face with sorrow. The savage beats his breast in an effort to fill the empty feeling left by sorrow. The saint knows the same sadness, but through the eyes of Christian faith he is convinced that every dark night is followed by a beautiful dawn. You may sail down the sea of life for many years without the slightest ripple in the calm water, but remember, soon or late, the storms come and the mighty waves cause the ship of life to lurch to and fro. These experiences test the anchors of faith and try our Christian skills.

Physical pain can be relieved by many of our wonderful drugs. Our loved ones can approach the sunset of life without unbearable pain. Yet, there is no pill or antibiotic that can ease the anguish, loneliness, and suffering of a broken heart.

It is comforting to remember that while no man walks through the sunshine all his life, God makes available a light of faith that keeps us from losing our way.

Grief is the price-tag we find on the bag of love. God made us in such a way that we can both love and respond to love; if man did not have this ability there would be no sorrow in the world. Therefore, it follows that those who love most usually bear the heaviest load of sorrow.

Grief mirrors the deep qualities of the human soul; it reveals the concern we have for those in distress; it expresses the compassion which the soul is capable of extending because it senses the spiritual worth of man. Sorrow is evidence that man is a product of God.

Alfred Tennyson wrote:

> I hold it true, whate'er befall;
> I feel it, when I sorrow most;
> 'Tis better to have loved and lost
> Than never to have loved at all.

I have come to the unswerving conclusion that the aching heart, no matter how great the hurt, is a mighty small price to pay for the joy, gladness, and love we know in life.

I know a young couple who, for six years, loved a little boy. His life was full of hope and promise. One day, he contracted an incurable disease, and death took him to the Father's house. The feeling of loss for the parents cannot be expressed by human lips. Their grief seemed more than they could bear. In spite of this, they would prefer bearing their sorrow and holding in their hearts precious memories than never to have loved and held that little boy. He brought them six of the happiest years of their lives.

We ought to remember that there is no immediate cure for grief. I do not believe that it is consistent with God's nature to relieve sorrow instantaneously. Therefore, we should not be embarrassed or ashamed to display in an emotional way the deep hurts of the heart. Do not be afraid to give expression to your sorrow; to do so helps break the nervous strain, and it brings some relief.

In the eleventh chapter of John's Gospel there is an interesting story concerning the raising of Lazarus from the dead. Jesus and Lazarus were good friends. When Lazarus became critically ill, Martha and Mary, the sisters of Lazarus, sent word to Jesus. Before Jesus reached Bethany, Lazarus died. The writer of John tells us, "Now Jesus loved Martha, and her sister, and Lazarus" (John 11:5). Mary and Martha were crushed with this great sorrow and when Jesus arrived, He found the Jews trying to comfort them.

Jesus was troubled when He found the Jews weeping. He asked, ". . . Where have ye laid him? They said unto him, Lord, come and see" (John 11:34). As Jesus walked toward the grave, He found it impossible to control His emotions. "Jesus wept" (John 11:35) as He neared the place where His friend was buried.

Why did Jesus weep? Jesus knew that in the matter of a few minutes He would replace the sorrow with unimagined joy. He would soon heal broken hearts by raising Lazarus from the dead. Perhaps Jesus was overcome with sorrow as He saw so many hearts filled with sadness. Every sensitive life is touched at the sight of many broken hearts. Too, Jesus may have been weeping because His friend had entered the heavenly glories of his eternal home, and now he would be called back into a world of hate, greed, and hardship. Jesus may have been weeping because Lazarus had already heard the perfect harmony of heavenly music, and must give up the goal of life, for a time, and become again a part of the music where discordant notes fill the song of earthly existence.

It seems strange that Jesus would weep. Yet, I am glad that He did. In this lovely story we see revealed some of the deep qualities of our Master. The fact that Jesus wept teaches us that sorrow is natural. There are those who proclaim, "If I had assurance, beyond any reasonable doubt, that there is life after death, sorrow as a result of death could be banished." This, of course, is not true. Jesus knew that life is eternal. There was no hesitation or question mark in the mind of Jesus when He said to Martha, ". . . I am the resurrection, and the life: he that believeth in me, though he were dead, yet, shall he live: And whosoever liveth and believeth in me shall never die. Believest thou this?" (John 11:25-26). Even the sure knowledge of eternal life will not take all the grief out of the human heart when we lose our loved ones. It is natural that we should want to hold on to those we love as long as we can.

In some measure, the fact that "Jesus wept" tells us that God's heart is moved when we feel the piercing pain of sorrow. The writer of Hebrews wrote, "For we have not an high priest which cannot be touched with the feeling of our infirmities . . ." (Hebrews 4:15). Here we get an insight into another facet of God's nature. He has compassion upon us. The hurt hearts and crushed hopes of man are not unnoticed by the Creator.

There are times in life when people seem to think that man is alone with his heavy load of sorrow. Have you ever felt like that? It seems, at times, that no one is near to help carry the load and keep man from stumbling. We forget that after every night comes the sunshine. Jesus experienced the dark and lonely hours of Gethsemane and trudged slowly up the hill of Calvary before Easter came.

Whatever else we learn, as we journey through life, we ought to come face to face with this truth: we cannot go through a room which is darker than those our Lord has gone through before us. Look at His life: He was born in a stable. When His birth was announced, evil men became jealous and set out to take His life. He faced more opposition than any man who ever lived. His temptations were intense. He did more good than all the kings who ever ruled and received less praise than the modern garbage collector. Jesus was subjected to all sorts of humiliation. False charges were brought against Him. He was despised, spat upon, and stoned. He was doubted, deserted, betrayed, and denied. He was mocked, beaten, and abused, and men laughed at Him. He was unjustly tried by perverted men and unmercifully sentenced to die on the cross. His hands and feet bore the marks of steel spikes and His side was pierced with a sword. Jesus lived about thirty-three years. No man has suffered more in body or spirit than our Lord. Therefore, it would be impossible for you and me to experience greater pain, to know more sorrow, to bear heavier burdens, or to pass through a darker room than did Jesus Christ. These words of the prophet seem to fit our Lord: "He is despised and rejected of men; a man of sorrows, and acquainted with grief; and we hid as it were our faces from him; he was despised, and we esteemed him not" (Isaiah 53:3).

The psalmist was aware of God's presence as he said, "O Lord, thou hast searched me, and known me. Thou knowest my down-sitting and mine uprising, thou understandeth my thought afar off . . . and art acquainted with all my ways" (Psalm 139:1-3). I am glad the psalmist said that God is acquainted with all our ways; it means that God knows when our hearts are broken.

I want to suggest four things that will be helpful when the human heart faces sorrow.

1. Commit your feelings to God in prayer. The soul is never out of place when it is found upon its knees in the presence of God. David endured some great tragedies in his life. Once he said, "The sorrows of hell compassed me about; In my distress I called upon the Lord, and cried to my God: and he did hear my voice out of his temple, and my cry did enter into his ears" (II Samuel 22:6-7). God hears the prayer of the broken heart.

When I was a young boy, it was always a thrill to go without shoes during the hot summer months. It was also cheaper that way. Many times I ran to my mother with a stubbed toe. Some-how, she had the magic power to ease the pain, but even if the pain did not go away, my mother's presence gave me the assur-ance that all was well. I think this is true also with God's presence. There is no question but what He can ease some of our hurt. I would be foolish, however, to indicate that God will take all the hurt away. The miracle is found in the fact that in spite of the hurt, God will give us the feeling of security that tells us in no uncertain terms that all is well.

After you have committed your feelings to God, I believe you can say with David, ". . . when I cried thou answeredst me, and strengthenedst me with strength in my soul" (Psalm 138:3). This is the place where we need courage and strength, in the soul.

2. Talk to some trusted and understanding friend about your sorrow. A lot of people come to see me. Many of them are not members of our church. Just the other day a lady called and said, "I called you once before; I don't know whether you re-member me or not, but I have read many things you have written. I am sorry to take up your time, but I wanted to talk to someone and I thought you would understand." Her life was heavy with sorrow. She shared her burden with me and we had a prayer on

the telephone. Before she put down the receiver she remarked, "You will never know how much these few minutes have meant to me." The lady did most of the talking, and I listened. You will find some relief simply in sharing your grief with some understanding and trusted friend.

3. Keep this vital truth clearly in mind: God will not let you down. He will give you the strength to face sorrow. I live by the philosophy that God will see His people through life's inevitabilities. Since there is no way around grief, I am convinced that God provides a way through it. This has been substantiated in the lives of other people. We see it more clearly in the life of Jesus. When Jesus faced the cross, it was His wish to avoid it. If, however, He stood true to His purpose, He could not evade it. God gave Him the strength to face the inevitable with unyielding courage.

Paul referred to his "thorn in the flesh"; he mentioned this in his prayers on several occasions. He tells us, "For this thing I besought the Lord thrice, that it might depart from me" (II Corinthians 12:8). I suppose that one could assume that Paul prayed fervently about this infirmity three times. God did not remove the thorn in the flesh for Paul; this was one of life's inevitabilities. God assured Paul that he could live with it. ". . . My grace is sufficient for thee . . ." (II Corinthians 12:9). It is impossible to be free from grief, but God will provide the strength to see a rainbow of peach-colored hues through the tears of sorrow.

4. Finally, when grief descends upon you, read with a believing heart the wonderful affirmations of faith and promises found in the Bible. The psalmist said, "I will say of the Lord, He is my refuge and my fortress: my God; in him will I trust" (Psalm 91:2). And, "I will lift up mine eyes unto the hills, from whence cometh my help. My help cometh from the Lord, which made heaven and earth. . . . The Lord shall preserve thy going out and thy coming in from this time forth, and even for evermore" (Psalm 121:1,2,8). Paul proclaimed, "For we know that if our earthly house of this tabernacle were dissolved, we have a building of God, an house not made with hands, eternal in the heavens" (II Corinthians 5:1). "The Lord is my shepherd; I shall not want" (Psalm 23:1). I read an interpretation of this verse which I like. Actually, it was a misquote. A little girl said, "The Lord is my shepherd; and

79

that's all I want." When we come to realize that the Lord is our Shepherd, looking after us and caring for us, that is all that is necessary to bring the heart comfort.

Before Jesus faced the cross, He confidently said to His disciples, "Let not your heart be troubled: ye believe in God, believe also in me. In my Father's house are many mansions: if it were not so, I would have told you. I go to prepare a place for you" (John 14:1-2). The Bible offers comfort to those who read it with faith.

Now, let me suggest some things we should guard against when sorrow comes. In every area of life a person must have some guards. Unless we stand watch over all of life, we fail to be responsible disciples who push back the boundaries of God's Kingdom.

1. Do not give way to excessive grief. By this, I do not mean that one should not weep; it is often through tears that one finds relief. I mean simply that we ought to make it our business to master sorrow. To store grief inwardly could seriously injure your health. I know a lovely lady whose heart was crushed because death claimed one she loved most. She has buried herself in a life of grief: her talents are dormant; her usefulness to society is stifled. She is alive only to herself and the sorrow her heart knows. Excessive grief makes life miserable and it will destroy your health as well as your peace of mind.

2. Do not sit and brood over your sorrow. You can cultivate grief, and it will master your life. Your loved ones would not want their passing to rob your life of joy. This is a time to face life with courage. The challenge here ought to be to try with all your power to live up to the highest ideals of the person you loved. Somewhere, I read the lines about a minister who lost his son. After the service he said, "Now I shall have to laugh twice as much"; and he did. When grief strikes, here is the time to think and act positively.

When David received word that his son Absalom was dead, he went to his room and wept. The soldiers of David had defeated the enemy and Absalom had been killed in the process. The writer of II Samuel tells us, "And the victory that day was turned into mourning unto all the people: for the people heard say that day how the king was grieved for his son" (II Samuel 19:2).

It was Joab who came to David and encouraged him to stop

brooding over his deep sorrow. There is one evident truth the people recognized. He could not be effective serving as their king unless he moved out of his idle chamber of grief. This is also true with us. We cannot do the work God has for us to do if we remain in the idle room of grief. After Joab's visit with David, he came out of his chamber and ". . . sat in the gate . . ." (II Samuel 19:8). David returned to Jerusalem and served as king until his death.

3. Do not advertise your grief. What I mean by this is do not look for sympathy from every person you meet; to do so is a symptom of an emotional disturbance. In addition, seeking sympathy will be inclined to cause you to exaggerate your sorrow. The wound of sorrow will heal more quickly if you share it with some understanding friend, then seek God's peace, and let the matter rest. To talk about it freely with all you meet will only serve to keep the wound open.

4. Do not complain to yourself about your sorrow. We see most of life through our human minds which entertain, most of the time, human hopes. God looks at life through divine eyes and with divine wisdom. He has intelligently planned the best for His people. Who are we to say that all the sorrow we have been called upon to bear is not the best for our souls? We can complain about our grief and it will fester in our lives and cause us to lose all our noble hopes. God never intended any sorrow to break the spirit and snuff out the torch of life by which we are able to see how to fulfill the purpose and plan of our lives.

An unknown author wrote:

> My life is but the weaving
> Between my God and me.
> I only choose the colors
> He weaveth steadily.
> Sometimes he weaveth sorrow
> And I in foolish pride,
> Forget he sees the upper
> And I the underside.

Our anxieties about death become more intense because we lack knowledge about this experience. Many people have mistaken ideas about death. Here is a question many people ask me, "Is death

painful?" Dr. R. W. Mackenna wrote concerning this question,
". . . I have fought death, and lost the battle, over the beds of
young men and women cut down in their prime; and I have watched
the old totter down the slope into twilight, and at the end, fall asleep
like children, and I can say, with a due sense of the importance
of this statement, that my experience has been that, however
much men and women may, when in the full vigor of health, fear
death, when the hour approaches, they face the end with calmness
and a serene mind."

It appears that we leave life, in some sense, as we entered it,
with no mental disturbance and physical distress. I have talked
with many people who have walked to the door of death and later
recovered. Invariably, they have said that death seemed like a
welcome experience; they felt that the desire to go on into death
would be equally as strong as the desire to move back to life
and health.

When the great British surgeon, Dr. John Hunter, faced death,
his last words were, "If I had the strength enough to hold a pen,
I would write how easy and pleasant a thing it is to die." Mother
Nature seems to have been wonderfully kind to have built in a
device which causes loss of consciousness to intervene when we
reach a certain degree of bodily pain. It would be almost impossible to journey through life without pain, but I believe when
we have reached the door of death, our pain and suffering will be
over.

Then, people experience intense grief because they look upon
death as a lonesome event. It is true, we are helpless in the presence
of death. The only thing that we can do is stand by and watch.
Death is God's plan and He is present in this experience. Before
you release the grip you have on your loved-one's hand, you may
be sure that he is in the arms of God. We sometimes forget that
each little family belongs to a larger family; that, of course, is
God's family and He is the Father. Do not feel for one moment
that death is a lonesome valley for the dead. They are never out
of sight of the lights that shine from the Father's house. The
psalmist said, "Yea, though I walk through the valley of the shadow
of death, I will fear no evil: for thou art with me; thy rod and
thy staff they comfort me" (Psalm 23:4).

82

Finally, sorrow sometimes becomes intense because of the unanswered questions about heaven. For example, I have stood beside the grave and heard people say something like this: "If I knew he is in heaven and not in some semi-conscious state, I could stand up and face this better." There are many theories about what happens as soon as one enters the door of death. The belief I find most reasonable and most satisfying is based upon the words of Jesus as He spoke to the dying thief. The penitent thief looked into the forgiving eyes of our Lord and said, ". . . Lord, remember me when thou comest into thy kingdom. And Jesus said unto him, Verily I say unto thee, To day shalt thou be with me in paradise" (Luke 23:42-43). This is one of the clearest windows through which we can look into the room of death.

Jesus did not say, "When the doors of heaven are opened and the dead shall rise from the grave, you shall have a place with Me." Jesus said, "*To day* shalt thou be with me in paradise." There can be no misunderstanding about such a short, clear, and concise statement. In other words, Jesus was saying, "As soon as the last breath leaves your mortal body you shall be transported immediately to the Father's house." These words from the dying lips of our Lord give us assurance that we shall enjoy immediate fellowship with Him beyond the grave. Death is not even a comma in the sentence of life. We live forever in His presence and as soon as death comes we shall be with Him.

Grief is an open sore in the heart and mind of a person. If we permit it to become infected, like an infected wound, it will endanger our mental, physical, and spiritual health. How are we to face sorrow? What can God do about it? I am going to suggest what I believe to be some practical aids in helping to deal with the immense and universal problem of grief.

1. Time will help to heal the hurts of the heart. Time alone will not heal grief completely, but it will help. I have seen a few people who were just as emotional and grief-stricken over the loss of a loved one aften ten years as they were the week of the funeral. These are, of course, unusual cases. What I want to get across is the idea that we must cooperate with time. Time, as it passes by, will help us to accept the fact that our loved ones are gone, and it will also enable us to get a true perspective of life.

I know a man who almost lost his faith in God and who became bitter because of the death of his mother. Several months after her death he said, "I would not want my mother to come back. I am glad she is at peace with God." When sorrow comes, let time do its work, with your Christian faith working in the process of healing the wound of sorrow.

2. Think of what you have gained, instead of what you have lost during grief. The tendency always is to dwell upon our burdens instead of our blessings and upon our defeats rather than our victories. I am sure God would be pleased to have His children look at the ocean of joys upon which we have sailed instead of the storms of grief we have endured.

I am willing to admit that when a loved one departs from the shores of earthly life, the loss is overwhelming; the loss cannot be replaced. The Christian faith makes no claim to erase grief. The saint is as sensitive to the sharp pangs of sorrow as the sinner.

I once had a professor who lost his son during World War II. As were so many others, the young man was in the prime of life. What a tragedy! He stood on the threshold of a life of usefulness and promise. Then, he volunteered to fight in the service of his country. The day his parents received the news that he was dead, an avalanche of sorrow fell upon their hearts. Many friends called that evening, and they continued to call throughout the weeks ahead.

Some friends stood or sat a few minutes in complete silence; they did not know what to say. Others said all they knew to say, "I'm sorry." Some went beyond this, and tried to comfort the distraught parents by saying, "He was a good boy, and he is in heaven. Be thankful that he is in heaven. Be thankful that he will no longer face the hardships of life." Though wounded deeply by grief, the father was already feeling the comfort of God's love and his thoughts dwelt upon his son's rich life.

"I wanted to say," remarked the professor, "that John had never tried to escape the struggles and hardships of life. He stood up to them and faced them with courage. I must admit," he continued, "that I did not find comfort in that approach."

"I did find comfort when a friend came," said my teacher, "and put his arms around my shoulder and spoke gently, 'Thank God, Bill, for the nineteen wonderful years you had with John. Thank God for the joy he brought to your life.' "

When death comes, let us thank God that He has given us such a wonderful relationship with our loved ones. Thank God that they have made us happy, and in some measure, we have brought sunshine to their lives. My professor and friend found comfort as he set his mind not upon his loss, but upon the things he had gained by having a son for nineteen years.

There are many loved ones and friends in my life that I do not want to give up. Yet, I know that someday they will be taken from me, or I shall be taken from them. In spite of this, the joy, peace, and love they have brought will far outweigh the sorrow my heart will know when I bid them farewell. I truly hope that my life will be such that my loved ones and friends can say the same about me. If they can, then I know my life will not have been lived in vain.

3. God is a traveling companion in sorrow. God made us in such a way that sorrow is our lot: as we have already seen, it is peculiar to man and it reveals his kinship to God. Still, there is something of a mystery about the sorrow which is caused by hardship and suffering. I do not know why Socrates lifted the cup of poison to his lips and died while his evil judges remained in office. I cannot explain why Jesus was crucified while the chief priests continued to serve, Pilate held his gubernatorial seat, and Herod continued to pollute a throne with flagrant injustices and ugly sins. I find it hard to understand why God's people, those who had proclaimed Him King, had to walk for three hundred years in the storms of torture and persecutions.

I do know this. Out of trouble, fear, persecution, and death, emerged the Christian church. I cannot explain by logic why we must endure pain, hardship, and sorrow. I do know, however, what Jesus, the brave and courageous soldiers of the early church, and a host of others found to be true, that God stands with His children during the storms of life.

4. Let God use your sorrow. In a church I once served there was a blacksmith. I enjoyed going to his shop and watching him work. He explained to me how to take a piece of iron and temper

it, to heat it, and then cool it. This process of heating and cooling a piece of iron gives it strength and toughness. In some sense, sorrow can temper the soul; however, sorrow does not always strengthen the soul. The result of sorrow depends upon man, not God. This truth is clearly evident in the following lines: "Two men looked through prison bars; one saw mud, and the other saw stars."

It is possible that God is making us stronger men and women as we feel the hard blows of sorrow. I believe Jesus was better prepared to face the cross after meeting temptation and facing opposition and disappointment. All the hard blows helped to prepare Him to face Calvary unafraid.

John Bunyan was locked up in Bedford jail; here, he spent many sunless hours of loneliness and solitude. We would all agree that Bunyan was a greater Bunyan because of this than if he had been free to roam the streets. The prison bars could not confine his soul and his mind.

J. R. Miller has reminded us that man is like a huge block of marble before a sculptor. In making something noble and worthwhile out of man there is much that needs to be cut away. As God cuts away selfishness, pride, greed, and other deadly evils in our lives, we begin to find our real purpose. As Michelangelo watched the falling pieces of marble fly under the heavy strokes of his mallet he could say, "As the marble wastes, the image grows." As man, with God's help, cuts away the worldly aspects of life, he begins to take on the image of God.

John Homer Miller, a Congregational minister in New England, tells about one of his friends who had to give up what promised to be a great and notable career in the church: at first, he was stunned; his faith was shaky. The question *why* kept coming up in his mind. "Why should this happen to me in the prime of life?" After a few months, his faith righted itself and he was able to see through the gloom. The people who visited him always left a little better than when they came. God did not take away his infirmities, He did something better; He used them not only to make the sickly man stronger, but to make other people better.

"Take care," wrote Alexander Maclaren, "that you do not waste your sorrows; that you do not let the precious gifts of disappointments, pain, loss, loneliness, ill health, or similar afflictions that come into your daily life mar you instead of mend you."

5. Spiritual peace and comfort can be found only in God. David said, "For thou art my lamp, O Lord: and the Lord will lighten my darkness" (II Samuel 22:29). God is the only true source of comfort that will bring permanent peace to the sorrowing heart.

When Jesus talked to His disciples about His death, the disciples were confused. Without Christ their future looked hopeless. He assured them that they would not be left alone in a world of tribulations to fight for themselves. "I will not leave you comfortless: I will come to you," said Jesus (John 14:18). This assures us that the broken heart can be comforted. This Comforter is constantly available.

There are many things I do not know about God. His mind will never be completely understood by finite minds. There are some things, however, that I am certain about the nature of God. I know that He loves us; I also know that He understands when our hearts are broken. Then, I know that He can heal a broken heart, because He has healed mine. God made us. He made us to be with Him. His house is the goal of our journey. In Him we find life, purpose, and peace.

E. Stanley Jones tells this story about Dr. Lincoln Ferris, whose wife had been infected by a doctor who had just attended a childbirth from a diseased mother. Dr. Ferris spent thirty thousand dollars to bring his wife back to health. In the process, he nearly lost his faith. He asked, "O God, why didn't You stop that doctor at the door?" One day, as he walked along a street, he heard God speak. God said, "Can't you say what Jesus said, '. . . Father, into thy hands I commend my spirit . . .'?" (Luke 23:46). Before he took another step, he uttered those words from the depths of his heart and his despair left and he was happy again. E. Stanley Jones comments, "He entered into life—without a limp."

Surrender your grief to God. In Him you can find peace. Do it now. Say, "O God, into thy hands I commit myself, my sorrow, and my future."

87

6 PRAYER:
Man's Search for God

JESUS MET THE problems of life with electrifying success. The disciples watched Him rebuke the wind and the raging water. At His command the storm ceased and there was a great calm. He knew the secret of facing disappointment and unrest with poise and cheer. Watching Him, the disciples grew eager to know how to meet the tests of their lives with the same spirit of cheerfulness, for they recognized that in every life there are winds of prejudice, selfishness, and jealousy and in every heart the raging waters of greed, envy, and strife place the soul in jeopardy.

Jesus had the key to situations of earthly trial, sorrow, and temptation; He was able to rescue Himself from the areas that become dangerous for the ordinary man. The disciples found themselves near the edge of spiritual disaster many times, but Jesus was never near the brink of chaos and hopelessness; when He came face to face with temptation, He walked with unswerving confidence to the voice of God. The disciples sought the same calm assurance they saw in their Lord. As did the disciples, man today often thinks how wonderful it would be if he had the power to calm the evil winds that blow in life and still the storms that trouble his soul.

The disciples must have asked themselves, "What is the secret of our Master?" Then, perhaps they remembered something Jesus was doing in which they had not been engaged. Jesus was forever going aside to pray. There were times when He went to the mountains; other times He remained behind and sent the disciples away while He prayed. Still other times He withdrew by Himself and prayed behind closed doors. I can imagine the disciples saying, "Perhaps His secret is prayer."

One day His followers saw Jesus at prayer, and when He had finished one of their number said unto Him, "Lord, teach us to pray" (Luke 11:1). It was at that moment that Jesus taught His disciples to pray the prayer that has been universally acclaimed the greatest ever to fall from the lips of man—the Lord's Prayer.

Through the ages, prayer has not been without its critics. There are those who say, "I do not believe in prayer." Yet for every one person who is skeptical I can find a thousand who live above the shadow of doubt; they know prayer works, because God has answered many of their prayers. Some persons have tried to explain prayer away in terms of psychology. Others have discredited prayer on the basis that it is not reasonable to assume that there is a God who hears every prayer uttered by the lips of man. God is not just a projection of human personality. Prayer is more than simply a figment of man's imagination. What may appear reasonable to the mind of God might look impossible and contradictory to man.

If prayer is not true, this fact would have been discovered by some noble and intelligent man of integrity, and prayer would have been renounced a long time ago. The spiritual world, which has been experienced in the hearts of men across the centuries, is not a baseless product of man's imagination. It is a real world, as real as the world in which we see, touch, hear, smell, and taste. Prayer is just as real as love and beauty.

Someone has asked, "How can we be sure prayer is real?"

My reply is, "How can we be sure anything is real?" Here are some tests that ascertain the reality of a thing. Does it remain the same? Does it have the support of many truthful and dependable people? Does it have its origin outside the mind of man? Prayer can stand these tests. It is always the same; many generations of truthful men have witnessed to its validity. It does not depend upon the mind of man for its existence.

For the Christian, it would be foolish to ask the question, "Do men need to pray?" We might as well ask, "Can man survive

89

without water, food, or air?" A person of average intelligence knows the answer to these questions. If we conclude that the answer to the following questions is in the affirmative, then we know that man cannot live successfully without prayer. Do we need God's forgiveness? Do we need additional strength to face life with cheer and hope? Do we need divine guidance as we journey down life's trail? It was Abraham Lincoln who said, "I have been driven many times to my knees by the overwhelming conviction that I had nowhere else to go. My own wisdom, and that of all about me, seemed insufficient for the day."

Sometimes the burdens of life become so heavy and the problems of life become so complex that the soul has no alternative; it must cry out for help, help that is both outside and greater than mere human strength. There are times in every life when all human advice and resources fail to satisfy the deep and perplexing longings of the soul. Divine counsel is the only answer. This was true with Job. I am convinced that God was "calling the signals" during Job's trying days. Look at the picture: his children were dead; his sheep and oxen were gone; he had lost his wealth and his health, but not his wisdom. His wife advised him to curse God and die. In all his sorrow and misery Job was able to utter his affirmation of faith in God's goodness, "Though he slay me, yet will I trust him" (Job 13:15).

It seems foolish for the average man with average strength to assume that he is both wise and strong enough to carry on without God's help. Some have lived by this philosophy. There is a story in the New Testament that tells about a man who built his house on the sands. It fell, and the fall was a great one. Jesus, the Son of God, who was aware of His relationship to God, did not live under the illusion that He was self-sufficient. He knew that He must pray not only for the wisdom to know what He ought to do, but also for the strength to be faithful. The fact that Jesus felt the need to pray magnifies in me the great need for the experience of prayer.

Jesus prayed for guidance when He selected His disciples. He prayed before He healed the sick. He prayed for strength when He saw the possibility of the cross, and He prayed while hanging on the cross.

90

Some time ago a person said to me in a joking way, "I am so busy I do not have time to pray." I said to him, "You had better stop doing so many good things that you neglect your prayer life." The tragedy is that this man's statement is true in many lives. People become so busy doing things that ought to be done that they forget to pray. We would all agree that Jesus led a busy life. People were constantly making demands upon His time and energy. Yet we read frequently in the New Testament that Jesus went into the wilderness or went into the mountains to pray.

It is not necessary to limit one's prayer life to the quiet and guarded periods at the beginning or the end of the day. We certainly should have a quiet time when we can be alone with God, but we ought to pray too as we drive down the road or sit waiting for lunch to be served. Offer a prayer for courage as you put on your shoes each morning, and ask God to give you a clean heart as you wash your face.

Some unknown poet wrote:

> Dear Lord, excuse my heavy boots,
>   My dungarees and cap,
> I'm praying on my way to work,
>   For I'm a working chap.
>
> The bus is just ahead, but, Lord,
>   I've surely time to pray
> For strength to be a better man
>   Than I was yesterday.

I recall the time several years ago when electric power was made available in my boyhood community. I watched workmen secure the poles in the ground and string the wires. My father had our house wired and, finally, the power was turned on. It was a wonderful experience. Every corner of the room was lighted. One man in our community refused to wire his house for he did not want the unsightly poles across his land. As a result his house stayed dim and dark at night, while other homes were well lighted. Electricity was available to him, but he refused to use it. Prayer is comparable to the situation of the electricity. Man's soul can remain dark if he fails to use the source of spiritual power.

After the power was turned on, all of my family asked, "How did we ever get along without electricity?" If you make use of God's power plant and light up the dark places in your life, you will ask, "How did we ever get along without God's help?"

Prayer is more miraculous than zooming satellites, more powerful than nuclear warheads, more exciting than a trip to the moon. All the ships that ever floated, all the armies that ever marched, all the planes that have ever flown cannot equal the power of prayer. It is the most powerful weapon ever to be placed within reach of the human soul. If the impulse of prayer is disciplined, consecrated, and used wisely, it can harness gripping fear, control lustful desire, dissolve malignant hatred, and bleach the checkered and sinful stains of our filthy souls.

What is prayer? Prayer is like a diamond; it has many facets. Prayer is standing in the presence of God. It is lifting the soul above the noise of earth, beyond the clamor of everyday events, to the throne of God. Prayer is man in search of God. At its best, prayer seeks only God and not His outward blessings.

I like to think of prayer as conversation with God, but this idea is more than talking to God about life and then saying, "Amen." You would never think of calling a friend on the telephone and asking a question and immediately putting down the receiver before the friend could answer your inquiry. It follows that when we pray we should not put down the receiver and say, "Good night," until God has had a chance to speak. There should always be a time at the end of every prayer when we could just be still and wait. Before your prayer is ended, always ask God this question, "What do you want to say to me?" I am convinced that God is ready to guide us; He is eager to show us the way. Many times God is waiting until we become still and tune our hearts to the divine frequency.

Some people seem to think that prayer is a time to parade our virtues before God. Therefore, we get God's attention in the same manner as the Pharisee who stood and prayed, saying, ". . . God, I thank thee, that I am not as other men are, extortioners, unjust, adulterers, or even as this publican" (Luke 18:11). The Pharisee was saying, "I have never taken anything from my fellow man unlawfully; I would not be dishonest. I have kept my desires under control; I have lived a pure life." Then he continued, "I fast twice in the week, I give tithes of all that I possess" (Luke 18:12). According to Jesus, this man's prayer was not justified. Prayer is not a time to tell God how good we have been; He knows that already.

Many men pray as if they think prayer is a time to beg, a time to ask God to give them health, happiness, and material blessings. We all sometimes beg God in our prayers for the desires of our hearts. Did it ever occur to you that God knows what is best for us and that the desires of our hearts might be the cause of our spiritual bankruptcy? "We ignorant of ourselves," wrote Shakespeare, "beg often our own harms, which the wise powers deny for our good; so we find profit by losing our prayers."

Someone wrote, "I asked for strength that I might achieve. I was made weak that I might learn humbly to obey. I asked for health that I might do greater things. I was given infirmity that I might do better things. I asked for riches that I might be happy. I was given poverty that I might be wise. I asked for power that I might have the praise of men. I was given weakness that I might feel the need of God. I asked for all things that I might enjoy life. I was given life that I might enjoy all things."

We may look upon prayer as a chance to inform God how He ought to run His universe. Here, we are doing a dangerous thing. We are substituting our wisdom for God's wisdom. We are placing the finite above the infinite. Some of us are ready to persist in order to obtain our goal. This type of praying is little more than tipping our hats to God.

Prayer at its lowest is seeking to get our own way in life. At its best it is seeking God's will for life. It is the process of reporting for duty. "At their lowest," wrote Harry Emerson Fosdick, "men pray crudely, ignorantly, bitterly: at their best, men pray intelligently, spiritually, and magnanimously." When we pray as God wants us to, we will learn to pray with George Matheson, "It is thee and not thy gifts I crave."

Sometimes I get the idea that people who pray in public, and we preachers do more of this than anyone else, feel that the most important thing about their prayers is the well-chosen words they use. I don't believe that God is interested in the words man uses as much as He is interested in the sincerity and motivating force behind the prayer. I believe God hears the sincere prayer of the man who can neither read nor write as quickly as He hears the prayer of the disciplined monk.

God understands the human heart. Our hearts usually speak more clearly to God than do our tongues. I like to remember the little lad named Johnny whose grandmother came for a visit one winter. Johnny heard his grandmother complaining about the bitter cold, and of her difficulty in keeping warm. When Johnny said his prayer at night, his mother overheard him. He said the usual prayer, but added a little postscript to God. Here is it, "God bless Mommy, Daddy, Sister, and all our friends, and please, dear God, make it hot for Grandma. Amen." God understood what was in that little boy's heart.

Jesus gave us some simple directions for prayer in His Sermon on the Mount. Among other things He said this: ". . . when thou prayest, enter into thy closet, and when thou hast shut thy door, pray to thy Father which is in secret . . ." (Matthew 6:6). In other words, Jesus was saying a man ought to undress his soul before God. We do this only when we are alone. Yet, it is not enough just to be by one's self. Our physical bodies can be in one place and our minds a thousand miles away. Any observing preacher knows this is true. Therefore, Jesus suggested that when we enter our "closet," we must take another step and shut the door, shut out the noise of the world, and let our thoughts concentrate upon God. A man cannot truly pray if he is thinking about the opportunities of tomorrow; neither can a woman pray while she is concerned with planning tomorrow's meals. Jesus knew this; therefore, He suggested that the wheels of business should be stopped and all the distractions of the world be left outside. This type of praying permits us to see ourselves as we really are; we come to recognize in the stillness of a situation such as ours the need for God's forgiveness. It also gives us a clear picture of God. We focus our attention upon Him. We come to know that God's power is more than equal to our needs.

During my childhood we always attended church. We also had a family altar. Many times I have knelt with my family at church or in the living room of our home for prayer. I have heard my father pray hundreds of times, but I do not remember ever hearing

94

my mother pray. I know I have seen her pray; but even if I had never seen her do so, no one would ever be able to convince me that she does not pray often. Her life is the best example that I have ever seen of a life centered in prayer. One could not live as my mother lives without an open line to the throne of God. Mother is one who enters her "closet," closes the door, and prays to the Father who sees and hears in secret. He has done for my mother exactly what Jesus said He would do; He has rewarded her openly.

Jesus made two statements about prayer which people often take out of context. By doing this, they miss the real meaning of prayer; they become confused about prayer and often lose their faith in God.

Jesus said, "Ask, and it shall be given you; seek, and ye shall find; knock, and it shall be opened unto you" (Matthew 7:7). On first glance, one might think that here is the key that opens the door to a full life, satisfying all the wishes of our hearts if we ask, seek, and knock. What did Jesus actually mean? Just a few minutes before He said this, He spoke these words: ". . . seek ye first the kingdom of God, and his righteousness . . ." (Matthew 6:33). All this time, Jesus was talking to the same people. I think the assumption is clear; the man who seeks God's Kingdom first for his life can expect to ask and receive; seek and find; knock and have the door opened. It ought to be said that a man who seeks God's Kingdom first will refuse to ask, seek, or knock in an effort to gain anything selfish.

Most of us emphasize the material side of life too much and too often we neglect the spiritual. Frequently we apply a material interpretation to the teachings of Jesus when we should be searching for the spiritual meaning. It is fallacious to assume that Jesus was talking about diamonds, mink, and fine automobiles when He invited us to ask, seek, and knock, or when He gave us the assurance that we would receive.

His statement tells us of a way of life that man needs. We cannot get along without God; therefore, *we ought to ask Him for help.* To ask is an expression of our dependence upon God. The simple requests that we make are evidence that human strength is not sufficient. To ask is also an expression of our faith in a God who is equal to our requests.

Life is a process of seeking. This process indicates to God that we are willing to try. The man who sits in an easy chair and waits for joy to come to him will be disappointed. There are times when we must seek happiness, peace, and spiritual assurance. We must often search for ways to solve our problems; God will not do for us the things which we can do for ourselves.

Jesus' statement illustrates a second undeniable truth: *we must knock.* There are many doors in life which we cannot open. Try as we may, the only thing we can do is knock. God must open the door. The other day a woman called me on the telephone and told me a very sad story. Her life was miserable; she needed someone to open some doors for her. But before she could have peace of mind, she had to knock on the door of forgiveness. She needed to forgive and be forgiven. Only God could open this door. Then, she needed to walk through the door of understanding. The woman had no regard for others. She understood her own little problem and had plenty of self-pity, but she had no sense of understanding regarding the wounds of another person involved. Before this unhappy individual could enjoy the bright sunshine of God's love and feel the gentle breeze of peace one knows only when all his relationships are Christian, she had to ask and to knock, and God had to open some doors.

Another truth which I see in Jesus' invitation to ask, seek, and knock is this. Jesus chose this way of revealing that *God responds to man's actual needs.* By our asking, we are assured that God will come to our rescue in time of stress. By seeking, we will surely find all that is necessary to live life as God wants us to live it. And our knocking opens doors which could not be opened with mere human strength and wisdom. On these doors one finds divine locks and only divine keys can open them.

When I responded to the call to preach, I was totally unprepared financially. I knew that a college education and theological training were necessary, and I knew also that my family would be able to help me very little, for at that time, my father's health was poor. He worked only as much as he was able, and we found the family budgeting pretty difficult. My mother had gone to work to help pay the bills. There was not enough money to pay my tuition, therefore I had to do some asking, seeking, and knocking. I feel sure that the day I left to go to college my father emptied his pockets and gave me all the money he had.

I asked God for an opportunity to go to college and against heavy odds I received that opportunity. I sought a job and found one in the school laundry. Later, I was privileged to serve as the pastor of six rural churches. I knocked and God opened doors for me that neither I nor those who loved me most could open.

Another statement made by Jesus which is often misinterpreted is this: "If ye shall ask any thing in my name, I will do it" (John 14:14). A casual reader might take this to be a blank check signed by Jesus on the Father's bank. All we are required to do is fill it out. I have heard some people misquote this statement.

Some have asked me, "Didn't Jesus say, 'ask *anything*, and I will do it'?"

My reply is, "No, Jesus didn't say that. He said, 'if ye shall ask any thing *in my name*, I will do it.'" There is a big difference between these two statements. Those three little words, "*in my name*," make the difference. What, then, did Jesus mean? He certainly did not mean for us to misuse prayer. He expects us to use intelligence and consecration when we pray. What can I ask in the name of Jesus? I could not look God in the face and pray in His name for anything that is of a selfish nature. I could ask, on the other hand, for anything that would help heal the hurts of the world. I could ask for anything that would make me a better person. I could ask Him to heal the wounds of misunderstanding, to cut away the malignant growth of selfishness. I could ask God to give me wisdom, patience, and a spirit akin to the spirit of Jesus. These are the things I could ask, in His name, and I believe He would grant them.

What do I want to accomplish through prayer? Here is an important question regarding prayer that every person ought to consider. In our best moments we would agree that we desire most of all fellowship with God and the wisdom to know His will for our lives. Could we not also agree that all our prayers do not reflect these purposes? Frequently, we insist upon getting our own way in life, yet our way is not always the way of God's will.

I believe our greatest need is to pray for ourselves. By this I do not mean for us to pray selfishly. On the other hand, I do not be-

97

lieve we can properly pray for others until we have prayed for ourselves, and in some measure have asked God to get us straightened out. Here are some rules to remember when we pray.

1. Begin with God. Many people begin prayer by thinking about their wishes, defeats, and troubles. Some begin their prayers in a mood of feeling sorry for themselves. Shut self out and begin with God. If we can learn to forget self and saturate our minds with thoughts about God, prayer will be more meaningful.

2. Thank God for His blessings. This helps us to develop a grateful heart. It takes our minds off our disappointments and failures and places our thoughts on God's unnumbered blessings. He has been better to all of us than we deserve, for we are the recipients of many blessings which we did not seek.

3. Pray that God will forgive our sins. Don't just pray, "God forgive my sins." Ask Him to forgive specific sins. Ask Him to forgive your lack of patience, your unkind words, your deliberate acts of evil. When we go to a friend and ask for help, we don't just say, "Help me." We tell him in some detail what we want him to do for us. You will discover that you feel better after you pray if you recall the names of those you may have offended. We must learn to forgive those who have hurt us, because this is the first step in experiencing God's forgiveness.

4. God's rules for prayer are the same for all; no person has any special privileges in prayer. God expects us to be sincere, humble, and penitent. We must come to Him with a believing heart. He wants us to make our requests known unto Him and then pray that His will may be done. Madame Chiang Kai-shek wrote, "I used to pray that God would do this or that. Now I pray that God will make His will known to me."

5. God wants His children to have the best. Jesus told us that God was like a good father. A good father is one who always tries to give his children the best in life. Our selfishness and lack of wisdom frequently rob us of God's blessings. God is looking out for His children; He strives to keep us from doing things which cause us to hurt ourselves.

6. The door to the Father's house is always ajar. You can go in and out of the Father's house through prayer at any hour of the day or night. I have a large room in the parsonage with a terrace entrance that I use for a study. In this room I have a large desk, a

conference-sized table, some easy chairs, and many books. When my son Randall, who is three years old, discovers that I am in the study, he is tempted to come in for a visit. It is difficult to prepare sermons when a little boy is constantly coming and going. My wife and I talked about this problem, and concluded there were two things I could do: I could lock the door and refuse to let Randall come in, or I could leave the door open and be interrupted many times each day. I decided to leave the door unlocked, and my son comes and goes when he wants to. He brings some of his little problems to me, which to him, by the way, are grave problems. He has never found the door locked. I want him always to feel free to come to me any time he wants to talk to me. I believe God wants the same relationship with His children; therefore, He leaves the door open. We can go in and out as we please.

7. God answers all our prayers. I received a letter some weeks ago from a lady who was in the hospital. She was mature in many ways, but she was still an infant in her prayer life. "I prayed," she wrote, "that God would cure me. I believed that He would. But He has let me down. God did not answer my prayer." I wrote to her, telling her that I do not believe God ever lets us down. He will not desert us. I also told her that God answered her prayer; He did not give her the answer she wanted but, nevertheless, He answered it.

I believe God answers prayer in three ways. First, more often than we deserve, God says yes to our prayers: He really does say yes. I dare say that every person who reads these lines can think of many prayers that God has answered in this way in his life. The more advanced we become in the schoolroom of prayer, the more Christian our prayers become.

Then, God answers some of our prayers in this fashion, "I cannot say either yes or no. I will do My part and if you will do yours the prayer will be answered in the affirmative. However, if you fail to do your part, the answer will be in the negative." Consider, for example, the college student who prays, asking God to let him pass an examination. Whether he passes or not will depend upon his effort and his willingness to help himself. What I am trying to say is that many times we can help God to answer our prayers. Often, His answer will depend upon you and me.

Finally, God says no to many of our prayers. No is just as much an answer to prayer as *yes*. Once a little girl prayed that Santa Claus would bring her a big doll for Christmas. The family was poor in material things and Santa Claus did not bring the doll to her. Some thoughtless person made this comment to the little girl, "God did not answer your prayer."

The girl replied, "Oh yes, He did! God said *No*." I am convinced that when God says *no*, He does so because our request would either do us harm, or else to answer in the affirmative would mean God would have to go against His own nature. God says *no* out of His unceasing love and great wisdom.

Prayer is God's greatest gift to the human family. Through prayer we can find our way through the troubles of life. We can find the strength for every burden. We can find forgiveness for all our sins. Such power cannot flow through lives that are only half-consecrated. There is an answer to all our problems, and if you have not found the answer to yours, why not pray about it?

7 HOPE:
The Beginning of Progress

ONE OF THE saddest lines in all the Bible is the pathetic cry of David: ". . . no man cared for my soul" (Psalm 142:4). David felt that he was alone in the world and no one loved him or cared for him. A great problem that many people have to face in life today is loneliness. One can feel alone in the midst of a thousand people.

I shall never forget the first time I stood in Times Square. It was late at night and thousands of people were tramping up and down the street. The lights were gay and bright, the automobiles and taxis were blowing their horns. In the midst of all this I suddenly felt alone; I suddenly became aware of the fact that I did not know a single person in New York City, and no one knew me. I felt, for a moment, as David did when he said, ". . . no man cared for my soul."

As a minister, I talk with a great many people who look at life through glasses of hopelessness. They are people who have lost the true and noble purpose of life. The future is blurred; they see only disappointment and defeat.

Once a man called me and I detected a note of urgency in his voice. "I need help," he said. He gave me his name and address and asked, "Will you come?" I drove to the address and found him in a hysterical condition. He lived in a sixty-thousand-dollar house. He was one of the top men in his company, being paid more than thirty thousand dollars a year. Because of his immoral life, he had become inefficient, and the company for which he worked dis-

charged him. In his despair, he had turned to drink. He had become
so repulsive that his family had left him. "I have no future," he
said. "I have come to a dead-end street. The only way out is suicide."
We talked for a long time. Among other things, I told him that
God never permits His children to get into a situation where the
only door out is suicide. I suggested, before I left, that he do four
things. First, call upon God. Once when David was facing many
troubles, people said about him, ". . . There is no help for him in
God . . ." (Psalm 3:2). We never get ourselves in a place where we
are beyond the help of God if we call upon Him. David never believed that he was beyond God's help. He said, "But thou, O Lord,
art a shield for me; my glory, and the lifter up of mine head. I
cried unto the Lord with my voice, and he heard me out of his
holy hill . . ." (Psalm 3:3-4).

The second thing I told the wealthy but despondent man was
this: "Seek God's forgiveness." I reminded him that God's forgiveness is contingent upon our willingness to forgive those who have
sinned against us. Once we meet the requirements of forgiveness,
God releases us from the grip of guilt. Jesus said, ". . . forgive, and
ye shall be forgiven" (Luke 6:37). In one of David's prayers, he
said, "For thou, Lord, art good, and ready to forgive; and plenteous
in mercy unto all them that call upon thee" (Psalm 86:5). God
never turns His back upon a man who is sincerely seeking forgiveness.

Next, I encouraged that man to ask God to reveal unto him His
will. Once, Jesus said, "Ask, and it shall be given you; seek, and ye
shall find; knock, and it shall be opened unto you" (Matthew 7:7).
I do not know of a more noble prayer than to ask God to reveal
His will unto us. The promise is that if we ask, we will receive, and
if we seek, we will find.

All along our complex highway systems, I have noticed little
information centers. The purpose of these is to help those who
travel, and to keep them on the right road. I have driven to New
England from Georgia many times. I do not even need a road map
to take this trip over the familiar roads. My family and I drove up
a few months ago, however, and it had been three years since we
had done so, so I asked a tourist service to help me plan the trip.
This service routed me over some of the new roads, ones that had

been constructed since our last trip. They knew the best roads to travel. Now, life is far more complex than our system of roads, and God is always in the information booth to give us direction when we call upon Him. He knows the best paths to travel through life, and if we follow His direction, we will never come to a dead-end street.

Finally, I advised the discouraged fellow to turn his life over to God. Many people have tried to live without God's help and all have failed. God is not only the source of life, but He is also the strength and purpose of life. Man is fooling himself when he thinks he can get along without God. You can no more build a worthwhile life without God than a fish can swim without water. Tolstoy expressed a universal law when he said, "God is He without whom one cannot live." Without God, life has no real purpose; life becomes happy and meaningful only as we place ourselves in His hands. We have become a restless generation. Instead of finding deep water for smooth sailing in our desire for material comforts, we have drifted into the perilous waters where jagged rocks can easily wreck the ship of life.

In America, we have become rich in the abundance of things and poor in our concern for others. To the rest of the world, we have become a material giant. In our best hours, we must admit that our spiritual lives are anemic compared to the life of our Lord and Master. We have all kinds of gadgets and appliances to help us live more comfortably, but they have failed to bring us peace of mind. We are spending more and more money on amusement, and yet we are haunted by a feeling of emptiness. Within the next few decades, we shall undoubtedly conquer the remaining barriers to outer space. This is one of the tragedies of the generation of which you and I are a part: We shall conquer outer space before we master inner space. All our scientific progress and material advances fail to make us better Christians.

Once a man came to Jesus and asked, ". . . what shall I do that I may inherit eternal life?" (Mark 10:17). Jesus encouraged him to live according to the commandments. The man answered, ". . . Master, all these have I observed from my youth" (Mark 10:20). Jesus could sense this man's problem. He was a slave to his possessions. Jesus gave him an invitation to become His disciple, but he refused. He wanted to have assurance of eternal life without the responsibility of a cross. Our way and God's way are frequently poles apart. Abundant living is not the result of living as we want to, but rather it is the fruit of taking up a cross and following the commandments of God. This man let his possessions possess him.

Look with me for a few moments at the disciples after the crucifixion of our Lord. Before this horrible experience, the disciples were ecstatically happy. Their hopes and aspirations were high. Then came the death of our Lord, the experience that shattered their hopes and crushed their dreams. The disciples were thrown into an abyss of utter hopelessness. The atmosphere was one of overwhelming despair. The only future they had was the memory of three wonderful years with Jesus.

As I contemplate this scene, I can hear John speaking to Peter. "It's hard to believe that Jesus is gone. Only a few months ago, we watched Him restore sight to a helpless blind man. And, do you remember the day we met the leper and Jesus touched him and immediately he was made whole? Now, all we have left are our crushed hopes and shattered dreams. What can we do?" Peter places his face in his hands and sits silently for a moment. Then he rubs his eyes and says, "Three years ago, we thought we had found the Messiah. He kindled in us the hope of a new Kingdom. Where is that Kingdom now? I'll tell you where it is. It's out there on Calvary's hill; dead, lifeless, gone. The memories are sweet, but you can't establish a new Kingdom on the victories of the past and the dead hopes of the future."

James interrupts Peter. "Do you remember, Peter, the day we were in the little boat, and in the middle of the night Jesus came walking upon the water? We were all frightened at this strange sight, but He calmed our fears. You stepped out of the little boat and started walking toward Jesus. Then, one day Jesus asked what we thought about Him, and you spoke for all of us when you said, 'Thou art the Christ, the son of the living God.' We loved Him so much, and He made us so happy. We shall never see Him again. No one will ever be as gentle and kind. He loved the outcast, the lonely, and healed the brokenhearted. Now, He is dead."

"Stop," shouts Peter. "I can't stand it. Let us stop talking about

Him. I want to try to get Him off my mind. There is only one thing I know to do. I am going to mend my nets, prepare the boats, and go fishing."

When we find ourselves in the room of hopelessness, it can mean two things. First, it can mean defeat; it can be the end of all that is good and worthwhile. Second, it can be the turning point in life; we can look up and see the light of God's love shining through the clouds of hopelessness.

God often calls us to service when we are in despair. Do you remember when Isaiah went to the temple and saw a vision of God? Isaiah saw his sins in the light of God's holiness and cried, "... Woe is me! for I am undone; because I am a man of unclean lips . . ." (Isaiah 6:5). It was in this condition that God found Isaiah, and before the vision was over, Isaiah responded to the challenge of God. "... Here am I," he said, "send me" (Isaiah 6:8). God lifted Isaiah from the room of despair to a place of hope, faith, and expectation.

I have never seen a person who was sufficiently wise or strong enough to walk from the cradle to the grave without help. It does not matter how much wealth, wisdom, or authority one may have. There are times when these are useless in guiding us safely through the storms of life.

In our family room there hangs a lovely clock. My wife winds it every eight days. As long as she remembers to wind the clock, it keeps perfect time; if it does not get the proper attention, after eight days it will begin to run slow and eventually the clock stops. Life is like that. The wheels of life begin to run slow, and the springs need re-winding with some degree of regularity; our spiritual energy must be renewed and our goals constantly examined.

One question we ought to ask ourselves is this: Why does the future look hopeless? To discover the answer to the question *why* would certainly give us a clue to a solution to our dismay. Some people become despondent because they lack faith in God. Others become sad because they do not get their own way in life. We never stop to think that our way may not be best for us; many never stop to analyze the consequences. We only know that we have a desire, and we want to satisfy that desire.

The miracle of Dunkirk will be remembered as long as men write history. The British Navy, using nearly one thousand ships of all kinds, large and small, rescued over three hundred thirty-five thousand men fighting Nazis soldiers. Almost all their equipment was lost. When Churchill made his report to Parliament on June 4, 1940, a few days after the evacuation of Dunkirk, he shouted with enthusiasm, "We shall never surrender."

After four years of disaster and disappointment, those fighting against the Nazis rule were still struggling. Churchill addressed Parliament again on June 18, 1940. In that address, he referred to what he called "The Battle of Britain."

"Upon this battle," said Churchill, "depends the survival of Christian civilization. If we do our duty, the life of the world may move forward into broad sunlit uplands. But, if we fail, then the whole world will sink into the abyss of a new dark age. Let us, therefore . . . so bear ourselves that if the British Empire and its Commonwealth last for a thousand years, men will say, 'This was their finest hour.'" This is an expression of determination that suggests victory to those who look at life through glasses clouded with hopelessness. The way we respond to what appears to be a hopeless situation could mean our utter defeat, or it could mean that men will say, "This was their finest hour." Surely, we can say this about Jesus as He hung on the cross and prayed, ". . . Father, forgive them; for they know not what they do . . ." (Luke 23:34).

Let me suggest five things to remember when we find ourselves in the dark room of hopelessness. For the sake of clarity, let me say here that when God enters human life, no situation is beyond His power to solve. Therefore, when we place our hand in His, no burden becomes too heavy, no sorrow too great, and no problem beyond a solution. First, man is weak. We should not be surprised when we find life so tangled and twisted that human wisdom cannot straighten it out. David pointed out that one of the great things about God is that," ". . . he knoweth our frame; he remembereth that we are dust" (Psalm 103:14). Human weakness, however, is no excuse for immoral living. While God knows that perfection is difficult to attain, most of us could live better lives than we now are living. The person who comes to recognize that he needs the help of God is ready to walk out of the darkness of futility. The psalmist prayed, "Have mercy upon me, O Lord; for I am weak . . ." (Psalm 6:2). No man will lift his voice to God as long as he is foolish enough to believe he can handle life with his own strength.

One day, I met a friend on the street. I was late for an appointment and scarcely had time to greet him. When I asked, "How are you?" he replied, "Not so well." I could tell by his voice that he was dejected. Several days later, I saw him again, and he was on top of the world.

"You remember," he began, "when we met on the street the other day?"

I replied that I did.

"Well," he continued, "I was down, and just about out. My life was getting out of hand. Since then, I have heard God speak to me, and now I have placed my life under new management." The prodigal son did not think about returning to the father's house until he discovered he was weak and his strength was unequal to the demands of life.

Once, while Jesus and His disciples were sailing across the sea, there arose a great storm. Jesus was asleep. The waves were so high it appeared the ship would sink. The disciples knew they were helpless. Their only hope was to cry out for their Lord to save them. Therefore, the disciples came to Jesus, ". . . and awoke him, saying, Lord, save us: we perish" (Matthew 8:25). What did Jesus do when He found His disciples frantically crying out for help? He spoke to them, ". . . Why are ye fearful, O ye of little faith?" (Matthew 8:26). In other words, Jesus was saying, "You do not need to be afraid; I am with you."

My first job in life was working in a little community store near my home. I remember walking home from the little country store after dark; it was only a short distance, yet I was afraid. Many times my father would come to the store about closing-time to walk home with me. I was never afraid as long as he was near.

There is a little chorus which I enjoyed singing as a lad in church school. The words of the song ring out an eternal truth which we need to discover as we journey down the path of life. The song goes something like this:

> Jesus loves me, this I know,
>   For the Bible tells me so.
> Little ones to Him belong,
>   They are weak, but He is strong.

When our strength seems to falter in the face of some of life's problems, we might do well to remember that we are weak, but He is strong.

When life looks hopeless, remember that we belong to God. In the very first chapter of the Bible, we find these words: "So God created man in his own image, in the image of God created he him; male and female created he them" (Genesis 1:27). We owe our existence to God. He formed us out of the dust of the ground and breathed into our nostrils the breath of life, and we became a living soul. The psalmist said, "The earth is the Lord's, and the fulness thereof; the world, and they that dwell therein" (Psalm 24:1).

I know a mother who has twenty-one children. Now that is a large family. It used to amuse me when I was young to hear her name her children; she could call all the names without a moment's hesitation. She knew and loved them all. It would be hard for me to conceive of a mother's forgetting a child; likewise, as we belong to God, I am confident that He remembers us and is interested in us.

To me, it is a wonderful idea to recognize that I belong to God. If I belong to the Creator of the universe, why should I ever be despondent? I can say to others and believe myself, the following words written by C. D. Martin:

> Be not dismayed whate'er betide,
>   God will take care of you.
> Beneath His wings of love abide,
>   God will take care of you.

Then, we should remember that God understands us. I believe God knows when we are disappointed. He understands when our hearts are aching with sorrow. The psalmist wrote, "The Lord knoweth the thoughts of man . . ." (Psalm 94:11).

Jesus once healed a sick man, and the scribes looked on and said among themselves, ". . . This man blasphemeth" (Matthew 9:3), and Jesus knew their thoughts. God knows when a sparrow falls, ". . . and not one of them is forgotten before God" (Luke 12:6). The psalmist reminds us of the greatness of God. "He healeth the broken in heart, and bindeth up their wounds. He telleth the number of the stars; he calleth them all by their names. Great is our Lord, and of great power: his understanding is infinite" (Psalm 147:3-5). Jesus tells us that God knows all about us. "But the very hairs on your head are all numbered" (Matthew 10:30).

The psalmist could scarcely fathom the worth of man. He looked all about him and saw the glory of God's world; the moon and stars. Then, he proclaimed, "What is man, that thou art mindful of him?" And, "For thou hast made him a little lower than the angels, and hast crowned him with glory and honour" (Psalm 8:4-5).

Today, we can see a million more stars through our powerful telescopes than the psalmist ever dreamed were in the heavens. Of all the millions of people who have ever lived and died, God understands me and is eager for me to love Him. Augustine said this about God: "He loves us every one as though there were but one of us to love."

When we come to believe that God understands even the secrets of our hearts, it is both a wonderful, and at the same time, a frightening thought. There is comfort in knowing that God knows when I am despondent. On the other hand, it is frustrating to discover that no sin, thought, or deed can be hidden from God.

In days of hopelessness, we should find comfort and courage in the fact that God is our Father. Jesus is the best portrait we have of God, and He taught us that God is like a father. He told us the story of the man who had two sons. One left home, and the other chose to stay at home. One received from his father all that was coming to him in the way of an inheritance. He foolishly wasted his money. When all his money was gone, he recognized his wretched condition and began to think of home. The prodigal son decided on a course of action.

First, he said, "I will arise . . ." (Luke 15:18). He was wasting his life in the far country. He knew that to sit in the land of utter despair would not help his situation. Therefore, he decided to do something about it. Second, he said to himself, I will ". . . go to my father . . ." (Luke 15:18). This was a wise choice. He could have gone to a friend, but he wanted to see his father; and somehow I believe the prodigal son knew that his father would understand. Third, he knew he had sinned and he wanted to be forgiven. Fourth, the wayward son was willing to serve. He said to himself, "I will say unto my father, '. . . make me as one of thy hired servants'" (Luke 15:19). He did not demand anything from his father; he just wanted to be restored as a servant in the father's house.

The story does not end here. There is a more thrilling chapter. This chapter gives us a clue to the nature of God. The father saw his son coming down the road and ran to meet him. The father ". . . fell on his neck, and kissed him" (Luke 15:20).

Let me suggest four attributes that a good father will possess. First, he is a friend. While watching television, I heard someone ask a little boy to name his best friend. He replied, "My dad is my best friend." A friend is one for whom we have affection and respect; you can trust a friend. God is our Father; therefore, He is our friend.

Second, a father always seeks the best for his children. My father wanted to be sure that each of his children went to school. When we were ill, he called a doctor. He took us to church, and we sat and worshiped together. He was completely unselfish and he always worked for the best interests of his children. God is like that.

Third, a father is interested in guiding his children. My greatest ambition is to have the wisdom to guide my son down the path of life that will eventually bring him to the Father's house. Nothing else in life is quite as important to me as this. I will do anything within my power to guide my son's footsteps, not so much over the easy road, but in the way which will fortify his soul and develop his life into the likeness of Jesus. Shakespeare wrote, "God shall be my hope, my stay, my guide and lantern to my feet."

Fourth, a devoted father will forgive his children. My son could do a great many things which would cause me great sorrow. There is one thing he can never do, and that is hurt me so deeply that I cannot find it in my heart to forgive him. Forgiveness is the fruit of love. Theodore Speers wrote, "How to forgive is something we have to learn; not as a duty or an obligation, but as an experience akin to the experience of love. It must come into being spontaneously." When you think about this statement in the light of the following words, you can begin to understand something about God's ability to forgive. "For God so loved the world, that he gave his only begotten Son, . . ." (John 3:16).

Roy Angell asked Sir Wilfred Grenfell once to tell him what influenced him to give himself so unreservedly to God. After a few moments of reflection, Dr. Grenfell spoke quietly and reverently, "Into the hospital where I was a resident physician, a woman terribly burned was brought one night. We all saw immediately that there was no hope for her. We discovered that her husband had come home drunk and thrown a paraffin lamp over her. We summoned the police, and when they arrived, they brought with them the half-sobered husband. The magistrate leaned over the bed and insisted that the patient tell the police exactly what happened. He tried to impress upon the woman the importance of telling the exact truth, since she had only an hour to live. She turned her face from side to side avoiding looking at her husband, who stood at the foot of the bed, a miserable creature. Finally, her eyes came to rest on his hands, and slowly raised to his face. The look of suffering disappeared from her face and in its place came one of tenderness, love, and all the beautiful things that a woman's face can express. She looked back then to the magistrate and said in a quiet, clear voice, 'Sir, it was just an accident,' and with a shadow of a smile still on her face, she snuggled down in the pillows and died."

Dr. Grenfell said that he went back to his room and sat for a long time in meditation. "Finally," he said, "I spoke out loud, 'This was like God and God is like that. His love sees through our sins.'"

A good father does forgive his children. To know that we can be forgiven of our sins is good news. God is in the forgiving business.

Finally, let us remember that God is greater than any situation in which we find ourselves. When Paul went to Macedonia, he tells us, to use his own words, ". . . without were fightings, within were fears" (II Corinthians 7:5). Paul probably met with opposition within the church as well as attacks from the pagan forces. He was inwardly depressed and outwardly harassed.

Then, Titus, who had been on a mission to the church at Corinth, returned and reported to Paul that the church at Corinth longed to see him and had promised to stand behind him with all the forces at their command. When Paul heard this good news, his outlook was immediately changed. He still had opposition: the struggle had not been lessened, but in all his trouble he said, "Nevertheless God, that comforteth those that are cast down, comforted us . . ." (II Corinthians 7:6).

The same power that was available to Paul is at our fingertips. God can give us the courage to say with Paul during days of hopelessness, ". . . I am exceeding joyful in all our tribulation" (II Corinthians 7:4).

The secret of overcoming the world is to give ourselves completely and without reservation to the will of God. John, in his first epistle, wrote, "For whatsoever is born of God overcometh the world . . ." (I John 5:4).

Jesus warned His disciples of the suffering that awaited them. This looked like utter defeat. Then, Jesus whispered something that we need to hear over and over again. ". . . be of good cheer; I have overcome the world" (John 16:33). Once, the disciples saw Jesus lose a battle. A man with whom Jesus had been talking turned his back and refused to become a follower. Actually the man who left Jesus was the defeated man. He turned away from all that could be called good and noble and walked toward his possessions. He was a rich man, and Jesus wanted the man to love God more than he loved his wealth.

As that man walked slowly away, Jesus said, "For it is easier for a camel to go through a needle's eye, than for a rich man to enter into the kingdom of God" (Luke 18:25).

For a moment, the disciples were stunned, and they asked, ". . . Who then can be saved?" (Luke 18:26).

Then Jesus said, ". . . The things which are impossible with men are possible with God" (Luke 18:27).

Jesus was saying, "You are weak, but God is strong. You are limited, but God is all-powerful. Your spiritual vision is obscure, but God sees clearly. There are some things in life which you cannot do, but God can accomplish His purpose where you fail." God tends to specialize in the impossible.

Take courage and say with me, "I do not have to sit in this chair of hopelessness; I am weak but God can do for me the things I am unable to do for myself. I belong to God, and He understands me. God is my Father, and He is greater than anything that can happen to me." When we come to know God as our Father, we can take off our glasses of hopelessness and look at life through the eyes of faith.

8 FAITH:

Light for Life When Things Go Wrong

I WRITE A column for several newspapers and magazines. As a result of this, many people write and tell me the stories of their confused and twisted lives. Somewhere in their letters most of them manage to ask, "Do you think there is help for me?" My reply is *yes*. I do not believe that any life is beyond God's power to rescue. God can unravel the tangled cords of any life and repair the broken strings of man's heart.

I know a man who has mastered the art of appearing poised, unruffled, and casual. He always looks as if he lives in the imaginary land of Utopia. I asked him one day how he learned to relax and meet the perplexing problems of life with so much confidence. He answered: "Under the cloak of apparent composure there are fears, frustrations, and a constant struggle." I suppose if one could lift up the superficial covering of most lives one would discover confusion and anxiety.

There are times in business, government, and our personal lives when things go wrong. In an essay Emerson wrote: "Every roof is agreeable to the eye until it is lifted: then we find tragedy. . . ." The question that remains unanswered in many hearts is this: "Is there light for living when things go wrong?"

Jesus lived a perfect life, but there were times when things did not go as He wished. By following the example of our Lord we can discover a flicker of light that will help guide us through times of uncertainty.

As Jesus turned toward His hometown, Nazareth, His heart must have been filled with expectation and joy. No doubt He looked forward with gladness to being able to visit with His mother and father. Many questions must have filled His mind as He neared the place of His youth. Will these people believe Me? Will they permit Me to do for their souls what needs to be done? Will they be able to see beyond the boy they once knew and become aware of what God wants them to see in Me?

Jesus did not discover the answers to these burning questions until the Sabbath, when He entered the synagogue and began to teach. He taught the people many truths which would bring joy indescribable to those who lived by them and faithfully followed His example. His message was so inspiring that the people were shocked. They asked: "Is not this the carpenter, the son of Mary, the brother of James, and Joses, and of Juda, and Simon? and are not his sisters here with us? And they were offended at him" (Mark 6:3).

It is almost impossible to imagine the heartache that Jesus felt as He walked into His own home town to find that the people He loved did not understand Him. He wanted to do something for these humble folk and they not only refused to accept His message, they expressed hostility and even contempt for Him. Jesus' morale must have been at a low ebb. He was discouraged. He did not expect such cynicism, to say nothing about the antagonistic insults.

I shall never forget the experience of leaving home to go away to college. It was my first time to be away from those I loved for any extended period. I was eager for knowledge, but sad at the thought of leaving the home in which I had been sheltered, guided, and showered with more love than I deserved.

My first week at school was difficult. I was torn between what I knew I must do and what I wanted to do. My heart told me to go home, but my head reminded me that an education was necessary if I wanted to be of service to others in God's ministry. As the sun sank below the western horizon each evening, my thoughts would run across the miles to the humble dwelling where lived those who loved me most. When Friday came, I decided to hitch-hike home. Another student, who owned a car, was going part of the way and he kindly permitted me to ride with him. I arrived home just after midnight. By the time I reached the front door my mother had it open. She may have been a little exasperated at seeing me home, but the joy my heart knew and the welcome I could see written all over my mother's face made it of no import. Needless to say, I received a royal welcome. That first weekend at home was exciting and I enjoyed a hero's welcome from the few people who lived in our community.

How marvelous it would have been if the people of Nazareth had accepted Jesus in this fashion. He held the key to eternal life; He could unlock the doors of despair and release His fellow towns-people from rooms of prejudice, fear, and hate. The people of Nazareth missed the greatest opportunity of their lives. Since that day, kings, presidents, queens, and the great from every land have visited Nazareth; but none could compare with the gentle Saviour whom the people rejected.

Notice what Jesus did when things went wrong. He was discouraged, but not paralyzed. He was disappointed, but not defeated. He was despondent, but not without hope. His dreams were at a low ebb, but not stagnant. His aspirations were blurred, but not blotted.

First, *Jesus refused to give up*. He did not see in this rejection a hopeless situation; He did not lose His spirit or zeal, but kept on with His ministry. The person who refuses to give up when things go wrong will march across valleys of despair to mountain peaks of sunshine.

Consider Robert Louis Stevenson. He was frail from his infancy to manhood. When he was eight years of age, he almost died of a gastric fever that left him extremely weak for many months. Much of his adult life was spent in search of a climate which would give him some relief from his poor health. Stevenson wrote for many years from his bed of pain, composing lines that have thrilled humanity and encouraged people to pick up their broken dreams and work toward a noble life. Stevenson knew what it meant to have a "broken hope for a pillow at night." After weathering one of the stormy periods of his life he wrote: "There stood at the wheel that unknown steersman whom we call God." As did Jesus, Stevenson refused to give up.

I am a great admirer of Thomas Edison. He is reputed to have said, "When everybody else is quitting on a problem, that is the time when I begin."

In its early stages, the first phonograph invented by Edison was unsatisfactory. The high tones were harsh to the ear and the low tones were muffled. Edison employed a person whose task was to perfect the instrument. The man worked tirelessly for two years, trying everything he could think of that might improve the situation. Finally he became discouraged and went to Edison with the intention of quitting. When he told Edison he wished to resign, in view of the fact that he had spent a large sum of money and had failed to get a single sign of favorable results, the great inventor said: "I believe that for every problem God has given us, He has a solution. We may not find it, but some day someone will. Go back and try a while longer." One factor contributing to Edison's success as an inventor was his unfaltering determination to keep going when things went wrong.

There is not much God can do with a person who is ready to abandon his hopes at the first sign of opposition. On the other hand, there are unlimited possibilities for the person who is willing to take God by the hand and walk confidently when things go wrong.

Second, *Jesus did what He could.* Even though Jesus was disappointed at His reception in Nazareth, He did everything He could to improve the situation. He went about teaching and ". . . he laid his hands upon a few sick folk, and healed them" (Mark 6:5).

In Florida, where I preached a series of services, I had the wonderful privilege of meeting an admirable lady whose body was withering away, but whose spirit was radiant with qualities buried deep within her soul. She greeted the host pastor and me with a smile such as you see on the face of one who has just received some joyful news. She could not lift her fingers; someone had to take care of her as if she were a little baby. "I have been in this condition for eight years," she said. "When I had the strength, I always went to church and tried to serve my Lord." At our leave-taking, the godly lady said: "I am praying that God will bless all your efforts and that you will have a good meeting." Her wonderful spirit and her sincere prayers inspired me to do everything I could possibly do to preach with divine conviction the good news of our Lord. The invalid could not come to the services; she could not even dial the telephone to encourage others to come, but she did what she could: she prayed.

Jesus was limited in what He could do in Nazareth. The writer of the story tells us that Jesus could do "no mighty work" in His hometown. I have an idea that Jesus wants to do some "mighty work" for us, but, like the people of Nazareth, we stand in His way. Because of our selfishness, stubbornness, and pride we block many blessings that God wants us to have. We are all blessed beyond our deserving and most of us know it.

I know many people who live by the philosophy, "If I can't do a job to perfection, I will not do anything." Some refuse to teach a church-school class or sing in the choir because they feel they might not be able to perform to perfection. This is a coward's philosophy. I have always believed that God chooses imperfect men and women who love Him and who are willing to dedicate themselves to His will to do His work. Emerson wrote: "God will not have His work made manifest by cowards."

No matter how depressing life becomes there is always something one can do about it. God never deserts us. Many people become despondent and look at life through glasses of despair because they fail to do what they can about their own situation. When a man sinks to the valley of refusing to do all he can about his own life, failure is just around the next curve.

When I was in grammar school, I frequently would ask my father to help me with my arithmetic. He was always glad to give me assistance, but he would ask, "Have you tried to work the problems yourself?" If I answered in the affirmative, he would always come to my rescue. God wants us to do everything we can do to live the good life and when things go wrong, He is near to supply the strength and courage we need.

In the film story, *Madame Curie*, there is an inspiring scene between Pierre and Madame Curie. They had worked faithfully on a project and after 487 experiments in the laboratory their problem was still unsolved; the answer was not even in sight. Pierre said, "It can't be done; it can't be done! Maybe in a hundred years it can be done, but never in our lifetime."

His wife responded by saying, "If it takes a hundred years, it will be a pity, but I dare not do less than work for it as long as

118

I have life." When things go wrong, we need the spirit of Madame Curie and Jesus. We may not find the answer to our situation, but we must work and do all we can about it as long as God gives us breath.

Finally, *Jesus could not do a great work among the villagers of His youth because of their lack of faith.* The author of this story reminds us that Jesus ". . . marvelled because of their unbelief . . ." (Mark 6:6).

I know a young man who has a brilliant mind and a wonderful family. He told me once that he believed God had called him to preach. He has declined the summons. He has rebelled against the church and is throwing his life away. Unless he changes, it will not be many years before he will present to God a weary body, a fruitless mind, a withered soul, and a wasted life. If this young man could regain his faith, God could use him in a mighty way. His lack of faith stands in God's way. The youth does not believe that he would be an effective minister. He has lost his faith both in himself and in God.

The absence of faith is an open invitation to fear, anxiety, and worry. Lack of faith will starve the soul and become a great wall which will keep us from walking in God's beautiful garden of confidence and trust. Let me suggest three things about faith that each of us can remember with profit.

1. Faith is the beginning of progress. You will never make a worthy contribution to civilization until you possess faith in God, faith in yourself, and faith in your fellow man. Christopher Columbus left the port of Palos to sail west with a bagful of faith. He believed there was a shorter route to the West that would save the ships of the sea both money and time. Orville and Wilbur Wright believed that they could invent an aeroplane which would fly through the air. Dr. Jonas E. Salk believed God had placed in this intelligent universe a vaccine to help curb the dreadful disease of polio. Faith is the first step we take as we leave the room of uncertainty to an unknown point on the spiritual compass.

The writer of Hebrews reminds us that faith is necessary if we please God. "But without faith it is impossible to please him: for he that cometh to God must believe that he is, and that he is a rewarder of them that diligently seek him" (Hebrews 11:6). I believe we grow spiritually according to the amount of faith we exercise in our daily lives.

Once as Jesus entered Capernaum a centurion came to Him in behalf of one of his servants. The man wanted Jesus to heal his servant. The centurion expressed a faith in Jesus by coming with the request that Jesus make his servant well. Jesus said to the centurion, ". . . I will come and heal him" (Matthew 8:7). The man replied, ". . . Lord, I am not worthy that thou shouldest come under my roof: but speak the word only, and my servant shall be healed" (Matthew 8:8).

This incident in Capernaum was the greatest expression of faith that Jesus had witnessed. He assured the man that his servant was healed. ". . . Go thy way," said Jesus, "and as thou hast believed, so be it done unto thee . . ." (Matthew 8:13). This is a clear example of how God blesses us according to the measure of our faith.

I like the words of one of Charles Wesley's hymns:

> Father, I stretch my hands to Thee;
>   No other help I know
> If Thou withdraw Thyself from me,
>   Ah: whither shall I go.

2. Live as if you believe in God and your faith will grow. Dr. Wilfred Grenfell encouraged people to "act on what faith you have," and do not fret about your lack of faith. Someone has written:

> Trust Him when dark doubts assail thee,
>   Trust Him when trust is small,
> Trust Him, when simply to trust Him
>   Is the hardest thing of all.

The trouble with many people is that they do not use their faith. We sometimes forget that God has placed within us the capacity for a great faith. Our faith in God begins to develop when we look with observing eyes around us. The orderliness of the universe gives expression to an intelligent Creator. The beauty of nature speaks to us about a God of virtue. The bounty of the earth reminds us that God loves us, provides for us, and cares for us. We discover that faith grows as we cultivate it by daily activity. I often tell people to use what faith they have, and instead of diminishing the supply, they will find that it multiplies.

A father brought his son to Jesus, according to a story in the New Testament, with the faint hope that Jesus would cure him. This man loved his son, and he was anxious for him to live a normal life. The boy was subject to convulsive seizures. The father told Jesus that the boy was possessed with a dumb spirit, "and whenever it seizes him it throws him down, he foams at the mouth, grinds his teeth, and turns rigid" (Mark 9:18, MOFFATT).

Jesus said, "Bring him to me" (Mark 9:19). One of the secrets of life is found in this little phrase, "Bring him to me." The boy had an attack before Jesus, and the father looked into the gentle face of the Galilean and said, "If you can do anything, have pity on us and help us." The father expressed his lack of faith in Jesus by beginning his plea with *if* you can. Before Jesus could help him, he had to turn his doubts into faith.

Jesus said to the father, ". . . If thou canst believe, all things are possible to him who believeth" (Mark 9:22-23). Jesus was simply telling him that He could help his son; but first, he must believe, or else his lack of faith would stand in the way.

The father did not have much faith. He wanted to believe more than anything else, but in all honesty he could not believe. Recently I sat with a father in a hospital waiting room while his son lay in critical condition. The doctors told the father that they did not believe the boy would live. The father said to me, "I will do anything if God will let my little boy live."

The father who stood before Jesus was also willing to do anything. He spoke, with trembling lips, words that came from an honest heart. ". . . I believe; help thou my unbelief" (Mark 9:24). This man was saying to God, "I want to believe that You can help my son. If my faith is not sufficient, make it strong enough so that my son can be healed."

I have often wondered what happened to the faith of this man so long ago after this wonderful experience. He must have been a man of strong faith the rest of his life, for he used what faith he had and by using it his faith multiplied.

3. Pray that God will make your faith grow. This is what the

anxious father did. He cried out, "Help my unbelief." I believe the man was asking Jesus to give him faith equal to the problem he faced. Alfred Tennyson, in writing about faith, called it "a beam in darkness: let it grow."

We pray for everything under the sun: We ask God to help us realize our hopes and dreams; we ask God to make us well when we are sick; we pray that God will come to our rescue when we are in trouble. Why not pray that God will make us strong in faith?

I do not have much confidence in a man's religion if he blames God for everything that happens in his life that he considers bad. I know a man who loses his faith in the goodness of God every time he faces disappointment or any unpleasant experience. This man needs to pray and ask God to enable him to grow a strong faith so that his daily litany is: "I believe in the goodness of God during the long dark nights of sorrow and failure as well as during the bright days of sunshine and victory."

It is impossible to solve a problem by denouncing God and refusing to believe in Him. Thomas à Kempis was writing about faith in God when he wrote: "I find nothing without Thee but unstableness and folly."

When Horace Bushnell was a student at Yale University, he was disturbed about his own relationship to God. His faith seemed to fail. One day in desperation he fell upon his knees and prayed, "O God, I believe there is an eternal difference between right and wrong, and I hereby give myself up to do the right and to refrain from the wrong. I believe that Thou dost exist, and if Thou canst hear my cry reveal Thyself to me. I pledge myself to do Thy will, and I make this pledge fully, freely, and forever." In this prayer Bushnell was saying to God, "Things have been going wrong for me and I would like to place my life under new management." God took Bushnell by the hand and made out of him one of the great prophets of the Christian faith.

In the Old Testament there is a thrilling story which I enjoy reading, one that glitters with truth. It is the account of Joseph's being sold by his brothers. This was a cruel thing to do. Jacob, the father of Joseph, loved him "more than all his children"; when his brothers recognized this fact they became jealous. Unless jealousy is mastered and defeated in life it grows into a monster called hate.

Jacob made a beautiful coat for Joseph. This was evidence of obvious favoritism; the other children of Jacob did not own a coat with as many beautiful colors. Joseph was hated by his brothers because their father expressed more affection for him than for all the rest. This was the excuse for their hatred. Hate never has a reason; at best it can only offer a few feeble excuses.

One day Jacob sent Joseph to the field, where his brothers cared for the flock. Jacob wanted to know if the boys were well, and the sheep safe. It seems to me that Joseph's brothers should have seen, in his coming to see if they were well, evidence that their father loved them too. However, when Joseph's brothers saw him coming toward them, they began to discuss ways to satisfy the evil hate in their hearts. Reuben, one of the brothers, did not share the ill-feeling against Joseph. One brother suggested that they take Joseph's life, but Reuben pleaded with them not to shed his blood; rather, he suggested that they put Joseph into a nearby pit. Reuben intended to rescue his brother later and take him back to Jacob. The others agreed upon the plan to put their brother in the pit. At that moment, however, a caravan of Ishmaelites approached and the brothers decided to sell Joseph. The transaction was completed and when the caravan moved on and finally reached Egypt, Joseph was sold to an Egyptian captain, Potiphar, an officer of Pharaoh. Joseph became such a faithful and trusted servant that the Egyptian placed him in complete charge of his house.

What did Joseph do when things went wrong? He could have let revenge sour his life. He could have become resentful and let hate grow against his brothers. Surely he thought about his father who loved him; he must have faced the possibility that he would never see his father again. In spite of all this, he did not try to escape his sad plight. He called upon all the courage and strength that was available to him in order to make the best of an unpleasant situation.

I believe the secret of Joseph's attitude is found in the little phrase, ". . . the Lord was with Joseph . . ." (Genesis 39:21). Even when things went wrong, Joseph never lost control of himself. He held his temper; he appeared confident; Joseph knew that no situation is without hope as long as the Lord is near.

Joseph was faithful to the best that he knew during his trying days of uncertainty. He served Potiphar, the Egyptian captain, with unequaled faithfulness. He made every possible attempt to do only that which would bring his master pleasure. He also resisted temptation. When Potiphar's wife made continuing efforts to get Joseph to lie with her, he refused. He did not want to sin against God, or lose favor with those who had confidence in him.

One day, Potiphar's wife found Joseph in the house alone and caught him by the coat sleeve and said, "Lie with me." Joseph left his coat and ran out of the house. In a fit of rage, Potiphar's wife took the coat and clutched it near her breast and screamed. The other servants came rushing into her room and she cried with a liar's tongue, Joseph ". . . came in unto me to lie with me, and I cried out with a loud voice; and . . . when he heard that I lifted up my voice and cried, . . . he left his garment with me, and fled, and got him out" (Genesis 39:14-15). This caused Joseph more trouble. He was cast into prison, but he continued to remain faithful to the best he knew.

While a prisoner, Joseph interpreted Pharaoh's dreams and became known as a very wise and good man. He was appointed to be in charge of Pharaoh's house. It was Joseph's responsibility to gather food during the seven years of plenty and save some for the famine which was to follow.

I once received a letter from a man whose life was so mixed up that he mentioned to me the possibility of suicide. He wrote, "Nothing in my life goes right any more. I have just lost my job and my family is leaving me. Since I am no good to anyone I have thought of taking my life." He was in a pretty bad situation. I wrote to him and told him to hang on to life and do his best to make something worthwhile out of what he had left. "Others," I said, "have been discouraged, and with God's help they have taken their broken dreams and used them as steppingstones back to a life of usefulness."

Joseph must have been despondent, but he never surrendered himself to his self-pity. As a good soldier he marched forward with undiminished hope during life's most difficult battles. Joseph learned that God can use all of life if man is willing to make room for God in his life. Listen to the thrilling words of Joseph as he looked back on his life. ". . . For God hath caused me to be fruitful in the land of my affliction" (Genesis 41:52).

Just because things appear to go wrong does not necessarily mean that life is hopeless. God often takes a life that has lost its lustre and looks defeated and molds out of it a noble life which sparkles with eternal truth. Joseph was sold as a slave, unloved and unwanted by his own brothers, and cast into prison because of the evil tongue of Potiphar's wife. Yet he remained faithful to God and God used him to save the starving thousands during the famine.

John was cast on the Isle of Patmos as an exile. While he was without earthly companions, he was conscious of the presence of God. Here he saw the throne of heaven. He wrote about that noble company of saints, ". . . These are they which came out of great tribulation, and have washed their robes, and made them white in the blood of the Lamb. Therefore are they before the throne of God, and serve him day and night in his temple: and he that sitteth on the throne shall dwell among them. They shall hunger no more, neither thirst any more; neither shall the sun light on them, nor any heat. For the Lamb which is in the midst of the throne shall feed them, and shall lead them unto living fountains of waters: and God shall wipe away all tears from their eyes" (Revelation 7:14-17).

Paul was cast into prison, but he continued to witness for Christ. From behind prison bars he wrote: "For to me to live is Christ, and to die is gain" (Philippians 1:21).

George Washington Carver fought against terrific odds to make something worthwhile out of his life. His life was a constant struggle. Doctor Carver's philosophy was this: "Let down your buckets where you are." He encouraged people to make the best of whatever life gave them.

Once Carver was offered a salary of $175,000 a year to work with Thomas A. Edison in his laboratory in New Jersey. This might have been a great temptation to many, but not to George Washington Carver. He declined Mr. Edison's offer. This is the reason he gave for refusing to leave Tuskegee: "I felt that God was not through with me yet in Tuskegee; there was still plenty of work to do for Him here."

We may not be able to change our situation in life, but I am con-

vinced that God can use us where we are if we will only dedicate
ourselves to Him. God can take our feeble efforts, our failures, and
even our afflictions and make them count for good if we are dedicated to His will. Then we can say with the psalmist: "For this
God is our God for ever and ever: he will be our guide even unto
death" (Psalm 48:14).